INDIANA HANDGUN LAW

A Practical User's Guide to Licensing, Reciprocity, Carry Limits, and Force, along with Questions & Answers

2005 Edition

by

Bryan Lee Ciyou, Esq.

A Publication of:

CIYOU & DIXON, P.C.
320 North Meridian Street, Suite 311
Indianapolis, Indiana 46204
Telephone: (317) 972-8000
Telecopier: (317) 955-7100
Web: www.indianahandgunlaw.com
E-Mail: indianahandgun.law@sbcglobal.net

سید - جری -

Copyright © 2004

by

Bryan Lee Ciyou

The 2005 Edition of *Indiana Handgun Law* is designed and written to provide educational information about carrying a handgun in Indiana and the use of force. It is sold with the express understanding that Bryan Lee Ciyou and/or Ciyou & Dixon, P.C. is/are not engaged, in any form whatsoever, in rendering legal opinions or advice or other professional service(s) to the reader about the material contained herein.

Although an accurate summary of Indiana law at the time researched and/or written, laws are subject to different interpretations and vast changes. Thus, this Book is in no way intended to supplant, or limit, the need for any reader to seek the services of a competent attorney to answer any specific questions.

This book includes legislation through the first session of the 108th Congress and the 2003 regular session of the 113th General Assembly.

ISBN: 0-9752828-0-8

PREFACE

> The U.S. Supreme Court has stated that the right of the people to keep and bear arms is not constitutional in nature, but a right that enures to the citizens because it existed before the Constitution. Instead, the 2nd Amendment exists to restrict the Congress from infringing this right.
> –*U.S. v. Cruikshank*, 92 U.S. 542, 591-592 (1875)

My interest in firearms has now spanned over thirty years, and encompasses both longguns and handguns.[1] Thus, it was a natural progression, after being admitted to the Indiana Bar, to follow and work on cases with firearms' issues.

Today, after a decade of private practice, I pride myself on having amassed what I consider to be the most comprehensive working knowledge of certain segments of firearms law of any person in the State of Indiana.[2] I have been guided along the way by the substantial caselaw of the Indiana[3] and federal appellate courts.

Unfortunately, I have found that Indiana does not have a reference guide addressing the limitations on the carry of a handgun, and related matters, with an Indiana unlimited handgun license.[4] Many states do have such manuals, although they vary in quality from excellent[5] to poor.[6]

This has presented a substantial problem for Indiana lawyers, licensees, police officers, and others involved with this field, as there has been no effective way to quickly research general handgun matters. More fundamentally and troubling, my experiences and observations have confirmed, time after time, that these individuals often only have vague understandings of the limits on carry of a handgun and the use of force in Indiana.

I came to fully appreciate the potential positive impact of Indiana having a specific handgun guide, when I learned of the large number of handgun permits issued in Indiana, which presently stands at a staggering 320,000 licenses,[7] all in a state with a population of approximately six million residents.[8]

Thus, I ultimately resolved to write *Indiana Handgun Law*.[9] My writing objective was seemingly simple once I committed to this project: write a book focusing on the practical, day-to-day information that licensees, and others in the field, need to know and understand in order to comply with the relevant law. What follows is my best attempt to meet this goal.

I wish to make clear that this Book is intended to assist interested persons in better understanding Indiana and federal law regarding ownership, possession, and carry of a handgun. *Indiana Handgun Law* is not intended to aid anyone in circumventing the law.

Ownership of a firearm is a tremendous right and responsibility—and it will only continue to be that way if the law is followed.

Bryan Lee Ciyou, March, 2004
Indianapolis, Indiana

For My Wife, Julie VanWinkle-Ciyou,

and My Parents, Robert L. and Joyce A. Ciyou

ACKNOWLEDGMENTS

To those who assisted me with this Book:

Julie C. Dixon
Chris Ingler
Vernon E. Lorenz

To those who have taught me so much about firearms and the matters covered in this Book:

Russ Elmore
Herb Hopkins
Rod Horner
Ray Saltzman
Frank Wefler

A special thanks to Rob Deaton for cover design.

TABLE OF CONTENTS

INTRODUCTION

> The hierarchy of Indiana law: "The law governing
> this state is declared to be: First. The Constitution
> of the United States and of this state. Second. All
> statutes of the general assembly of the state in
> force, and not inconsistent with such constitutions.
> Third. All statutes of the United States in force, and
> relating to subjects over which congress has power
> to legislate for states, and not inconsistent with the
> Constitution of the United States. Fourth. The
> common law of England . . . ."
> –Indiana Code 1-1-2-1

This Book begins with an explanation of the relatively technical and complex means by which statutes, rules, and regulations come to exist as law[10] in the various states and the United States of America.[11]

A working understanding of the process is critical to the licensee in contemplating and identifying sources of law impacting his/her handgun carry. Additionally, a basic grasp of the law-making process will enable the licensee to better understand how existing laws are likely to be applied and/or interpreted in a given factual context.

Statutes, rules, and regulations are typically driven by underlying public policy and events.[12] For example, following the events of September 11, 2001, the underlying policy advocated on the state and federal level was to make the Nation, and its various states, "hardened target(s)" against acts of terrorism.[13]

This policy ultimately manifested itself in the law-making process, such as when the United States Congress[14] created

1

the Department of Homeland Security (DHS),[15] to provide for comprehensive domestic security, and enacted criminal laws regarding terrorist acts against mass transportation.[16]

Moreover, when any policy is to be advocated in the form of law, it must work within a complex hierarchy of laws, which exist at both the state and federal level. The foundational source of law in such hierarchies is constitutional, the supreme source of law from which all other law emanates.[17]

Firearms laws are typically constrained by these constitutional parameters. The Second Amendment[18] to the United States Constitution[19] is the ultimate federal source of firearms law. At the State level, Article I, § 32, of the Indiana Constitution, provides the constitutional right for those in Indiana to keep and bear arms.[20]

Specifically, with respect to gun laws, the Congress and the various state legislatures typically respond to an event by taking the policy to be advocated and then enacting statutory laws, criminal and/or civil,[21] all of which must fit within this constitutional authority. The judiciary then enforces, applies, and/or interprets these statutes, rules, and regulations.[22]

> [?] **EXAMPLE, Public Policy to Law Creation:** The policy advocated by the Indiana General Assembly,[23] post-September 11, 2001, was to make Indiana safe against terrorist attacks. One part of doing so was to encourage aggressive measures to mitigate any such plot. To further this policy, the Legislature enacted an air-piracy statute which, among other things, provides a criminal defendant with an affirmative criminal defense[24] for the use of force, including

deadly force, against any person terrorizing any flight over Indiana airspace.[25]

The foregoing noted, certain issues, including those related to firearms, require regulation in specific contexts and precise rule-making for which state and/or federal legislative bodies are often too slow to respond or ill-equipped to address. Generally, the separation of powers of the branches of government does not preclude state and federal legislative bodies from creating administrative bodies to do this work through statutory delegation.[26]

In fact, the Congress and the Legislature routinely meet their goals by statutorily creating such agencies, which, in turn, then enact rules and regulations that effectuate the legislative and political agendas.[27] It must be remembered, however, that administrative agencies only have the authority delegated to them by the grants of the Congress and Legislature.[28] Examples of administrative agencies that have adopted rules regarding firearms are the Indiana Gaming Commission[29] and the United States Post Office.[30]

Finally, the licensee must be cognizant of the right of any interest holder of private real property to effectively do as he/she wishes with the property. This allows private regulation of handguns on such property.[31]

These constitutional constraints, other laws, rules, regulations, and property rights, frame the bewildering array of considerations each licensee faces in carrying a handgun in every place, context, and time. Failure to consider all of these potential limitations places the licensee at extreme risk of civil suit, confiscation of the weapon, and/or criminal arrest, prosecution, and conviction.

Lest the reader believe this is over-reaching and alarmist, examples will be provided that show this is exactly what has happened to seemingly compliant licensees.[32]

Given the objectives of *Indiana Handgun Law* stated in the Preface, and potential sources of regulation noted in the Introduction, this Book covers the following topics, each of which has a dedicated chapter of consideration and analysis:

Licensing:

- Carrying a Handgun Without a License

- Handgun Licensing

- Handgun License Reciprocity

Carry Restrictions:

- Penal and Juvenile Facilities

- Schools, Buses, and Functions

- Airports and Airplanes

- State Fairgrounds

- Riverboat Casinos

- Maritime Ports

- State Courthouses and/or Courtrooms

- Federal Property

- Mass Transportation

- Private Property

Force:

- Use of Force

- Response to the Use of Force

It is hoped that these chapters, and the various [?] examples, [!]cautions, and [†] practical tips provided throughout, together with the question and answer section, will provide every Indiana licensee with the background to ask questions, obtain answers, and ultimately, follow the law.

In short, lawfully carrying a handgun is a serious matter that requires careful consideration. It is hoped that *Indiana Handgun Law* assists in this process.

5

PART I:
CARRYING A HANDGUN

> "The people shall have a right to bear arms, for the defense of themselves and the State."
> –Article I § 32, Indiana Constitution

Indiana is one of the several states that has a constitutional right to keep and bear arms.[33] The Indiana Constitution is clearly recognized by the Courts and Legislature as the supreme and foundational source of Indiana law.[34]

However, even with this constitutional right, the Courts have consistently ruled that Article I § 32 of the Indiana Constitution allows the Legislature to enact reasonable regulations for the use and possession of firearms, particularly handguns.[35]

Such judicial construction is consistent with the Legislature's inherent authority and its charge to regulate public safety and welfare.[36] The Legislature has utilized this power, enacting numerous criminal and civil statutes regarding firearms, perhaps most notably the requirement that an individual must be licensed to carry a handgun.[37]

Indiana Handgun Law, Chapter 1, addresses the Legislature's general criminal statutory prohibition against carrying a handgun without a license.[38] It then analyzes the licensing exceptions applicable to Indiana citizens as a whole, for carry in certain specific places.[39] Finally, this chapter concludes with a discussion of persons who are completely excluded from this criminal prohibition and the requirements of licensing.[40]

Chapter 2 discusses the handgun permit itself, focusing on the two types of Indiana licenses: (1) an unlimited license, and (2) a qualified license.[41] The balance of the chapter covers related matters, ranging from the application process for a license[42] to suspension and revocation.[43]

Part I concludes in Chapter 3, by addressing Indiana's reciprocity statute.[44] This statute recognizes other states' handgun licenses as valid in Indiana. Similarly, the laws of several other states recognize Indiana's handgun license. With reciprocal carry in a foreign state comes special problems and concerns for the Indiana licensee.

Chapter 1

Carrying a Handgun Without a License

> "I am troubled that Robertson is transformed from a law-abiding citizen one moment into a misdemeanant the next by merely stepping a few feet outside his [apartment] doorway while the handgun is still in his possession."
> –*Robertson v. State*, 765 N.E.2d 138, 140 (Ind. 2002)

I.   Introduction.

In Indiana, it is a criminal act to carry a handgun without an Indiana-issued license.[45] However, the Legislature has excepted from licensing the carrying[46] of a handgun in certain specific places and contexts.[47]

These exceptions are a likely acknowledgment of the outside limitations of government to interfere with certain constitutional and fundamental rights.[48]   These rights are: (1) private interests in real property, (2) the sanctity of the home place and family, and (3) the necessities of business.

Specifically, and assuming a handgun is lawfully possessed, the Legislature has created the following two penal code [49] exceptions to the criminal prohibition   against carrying a handgun without a license: (1) carrying a handgun in a person's dwelling, and (2) carrying on the person's property or fixed place of business.[50]

[!] CAUTION,   Carry Outside Dwelling: Lawfully carrying a handgun outside of one's dwelling is a very risky proposition, at best. The possessor would have to carefully verify that he/she fell within one of the statutory places that are exceptions to licensing, or transport the handgun in a "secure wrapper". The risk for a possessor needing to carry a handgun outside his/her dwelling, with any frequency, is grave compared to the minimal inconvenience and expense of obtaining a handgun license, all due to the criminal exposure from improper and illegal carry and/or transportation of the handgun. A handgun owner, thus, is always advised to obtain a license.

These two statutory exceptions (dwelling and property or fixed place of business) to licensing have existed in essentially the same form for a number of years.[51] Furthermore, what constitutes the "carrying" of a handgun, and the exception for possession of a handgun in a person's dwelling, have been substantially developed by the caselaw of the Courts.

It is important to note that regardless of these exceptions to licensing, a person who has been convicted of domestic battery [52] or who is a serious violent felon[53] is precluded from their application in all circumstances.[54]

> **[?] EXAMPLE, Domestic Battery Preclusion:** *Facts:* Joyce lives alone, and keeps a handgun in her home for her personal protection. The handgun is always locked in her desk, and never taken outside. She obtained it before she was convicted of domestic battery. Her home catches on fire, and the police department and fire department respond. A police officer finds the handgun in the burned out home. Joyce acknowledges it is hers, and explains she never takes it outside. She is charged. *Question:* Should Joyce be

convicted? *Answer:* Most likely, although additional facts are needed. There is a blanket prohibition against possession or carrying of a handgun, under any circumstance, by a person with a conviction for domestic battery, unless and until that person's rights are restored.[55]

Finally, there are a number of persons who are completely exempted from this statutory criminal scheme. These persons do not have to be licensed to carry a handgun, and include individuals such as police officers, other law enforcement officers,[56] judges, and private employees of certain express companies.[57]

This exemption, unlike those focused on handgun carry in a specific place and context (dwelling and property or fixed place of business), comes from the inherent nature and need of the person's job and legal standing. Any person believing they are exempted, should always consult with counsel for their respective trade group or professional association to make sure this is the case and to verify the current legal status of his/her standing.

II.   Selected Statutory Text.

". . .a person shall not carry a handgun in any vehicle or on or about the person's body. . .except in the person's dwelling, on the person's property or fixed place of business, without a license. . . ."[58]

III.   Crime and Punishment.

A.   Crime.

Unless excepted by place (dwelling and property or fixed place of business)[59] or exempted by vocation and/or legal standing (police officer) from licensing,[60] a person found carrying a handgun without a license is subject to arrest, prosecution, and conviction of a Class A misdemeanor.[61]

B.   Burden of Proof.

With this crime, the prosecution has the burden to prove, beyond a reasonable doubt, that a defendant carried a handgun on or about his/her person, away from his/her dwelling, property or fixed place of business.[62] If the prosecution meets its legal showing, then the burden shifts to the defendant.[63]

C.   Defenses.

If the burden of proof shifts, the defendant has the burden of proof to show an exception to the licensing statute.[64] This showing may be met in a variety of ways, including the defendant had a license,[65] the weapon was in a "secure wrapper",[66] or the weapon was not being carried.[67]

It is well to note that the line of demarcation between a general defense and an affirmative defense is blurred and may be overlapping. Specifically, some affirmative defenses may actually negate an element of the crime.[68]

The most common defense that a defendant asserts, is that he/she was not "carrying" the gun, negating an element of the crime.

D.   Punishment.

If convicted of the crime, and as noted, carrying of a handgun without a license is a Class A misdemeanor.[69] A Class A misdemeanor carries a presumptive prison sentence of up to one year of incarceration.[70]

However, this crime has several statutory enhancements, which make the crime and punishment more severe under certain circumstances. For example, the offense of carrying a handgun without a license is a Class C felony if it is committed on school property.[71]

IV.   Carry on the Person.

With regard to what constitutes "carrying" a handgun, there is a critical distinction between the ordinary, everyday understanding of this term and its legal meaning.   More specifically, the Courts have long held that the "carrying" of a handgun encompasses much more than just moving about with a firearm attached to one's body.[72]

A.   Ways to Carry a Handgun.

Specifically, there are two ways a person can "carry" a handgun: (1) on, or (2) about the person's body.[73]

1.   Actual Carry.

The first is the actual carrying of a handgun, which is "on" a person's body. This is where the person has direct physical control over the weapon, such as where it is stuck in a person's waistband.[74]

2.   Constructive Possession.

The second type of carry is by constructive possession, "about" the person's body. This occurs when a person has the intent and capability to maintain control over the handgun, presently, such as when it is under a person's car seat.[75]

When constructive possession is the theory of prosecution for carry of a handgun without a license, the prosecution must demonstrate the defendant's knowledge of the presence of the handgun.[76]

The defendant's knowledge may be (1) inferred from the exclusive dominion and control over the premise/vehicle containing the weapon, or (2) where the control is non-exclusive, by submission of additional circumstances pointing to the defendant's knowledge of the presence of the handgun.[77]

B.   Carry is a Question of Fact.

Determination of what constitutes the carrying and/or constructive possession of a handgun depends upon the facts and the circumstances of each situation.[78] Actual carry, or constructive possession of a handgun, without a license, is the same crime.[79]

Any person involved with, or who is around handguns, therefore, must be aware of what constitutes actual carry, and particularly of constructive possession, in order to avoid criminal exposure.

Indiana's trial courts and their juries are not inclined to acquit a defendant just because he/she does not physically have the handgun hidden on his/her body, as to do so would simply reward a clever criminal.

[?] EXAMPLE, Actual Carry or Constructive Possession:
Facts: Joe has his handgun collection stored in his rented,

drive-in storage unit. He is arrested at another location on an unrelated marijuana charge. His handguns are then found in his storage unit by police officers, subsequent and incident to his arrest. Joe is charged with carrying a handgun without a license, based on the guns found in his storage unit. *Question:* Should Joe be convicted of carrying a handgun without a license? *Answer:* No. There is no actual carry or constructive possession of the handguns.[80]

V.   Carry in Dwelling.

The threshold issue regarding a handgun in a dwelling, obviously, is whether the person was in present control of the handgun, by actually carrying the handgun on one's body or through constructive possession.

A.   Definition of Dwelling.

Assuming that carry is established, the possession must be only in the person's dwelling. Unfortunately, the Legislature did not define the term "dwelling" within the criminal article encompassing weapons.[81]   However, other provisions of the penal code do define this term.[82]

This definition, moreover, specifically mandates that it applies throughout the entire penal code.[83] The Courts have narrowly interpreted this definition of the term "dwelling" when applied to this exception for licensing,[84] despite the fact that the statute's express language is broad and includes "a . . . temporary . . . place of lodging."[85]

B.   Inside Home/Apartment Limit.

What appears to be clear law, where a license is not required at one's dwelling, only applies inside a person's home or apartment, while, and if, living there.

Any area outside one's apartment, literally, one step outside, is a common area of the person's apartment building (and not a part of the apartment) where a license is required.[86] The area outside of one's home may fall within the exception for property.

C.   Grey Areas Under Dwelling Exception.

Consistent with this rather strict interpretation, it would appear that there are many "grey" areas of concern and potential criminal risk for a possessor of a handgun, without a valid permit, under this dwelling exception.

A hotel room, for instance, would not be considered a temporary dwelling, unless there is clear evidence that the handgun possessor had registered in, paid for, and had done other things consistent with staying in a hotel, such as showering at, dressing within, and sleeping in the room.[87]

A prior living place, one to which a person still has even a strong tie, where the person may occasionally spend the night, such as at one's parent's house, likely also would not be permissible under this exception.[88]

In summary, the carry of a handgun in any area outside one's established home or apartment, generally, requires a license.

[?] EXAMPLE, What Constitutes a Dwelling: *Facts:* Mary is at a party in a hotel room with her boyfriend. Mary becomes intoxicated and begins to fight and yell at her boyfriend. The police are called by the hotel staff. As the police officers approach the hotel room door, they hear the slide of a pistol "racking" a round. Upon entry, the police officers discover a loaded handgun hidden between the box springs and mattress. Mary admits it is her weapon. Mary is then arrested for carrying a handgun without a license. *Question:* Should Mary be convicted of this crime? *Answer:* Yes, unless she can establish, from an evidentiary and factual standpoint, this was her temporary dwelling.[89]

VI. Carry on Person's Property.

The scope and application of the Legislature's exception for carrying a handgun on a person's property are not well developed. However, for conduct to constitute a violation of Indiana law, there would first have to be carry of the handgun.[90]

A. Definition of Property.

Unfortunately, as with the term "dwelling", the Legislature did not define the term "property" within this criminal article regarding weapons.[91]

There is, however, a rather broad definition of property found in the penal code.[92] It is reasonably certain that the Courts ultimately will not apply this definition due to legislative intent.[93]

B.   Real Property Interest Limitation.

Most likely and logically, a person's property will be interpreted to be real property interests, owned or leased.[94] Thus, a person owning/leasing a home should be entitled to carry a handgun both inside and outside the dwelling. But an apartment dweller only possesses, through the lease, the property inside the apartment itself,[95] and not in common areas.

Also, this exception should extend to undeveloped lots or tracts of land, or other real property that is owned or leased by a person. However, this property exception would not likely extend to the legal right to do an act on real property by virtue of a license (this license is not to be confused with a handgun license).

> [?] **EXAMPLE, Limits of Property:**   *Facts:* Ted hears a noise outside his home. He takes his pistol with him to investigate. Ultimately, he shoots and kills a burglar in the alley behind his home. The shooting is a legally justified use of deadly force.   Ted is charged with carrying a handgun without a license. *Question:* Should Ted be convicted of this crime? *Answer:* Yes. A public alley is not a part of his dwelling and/or real property.[96]

VII.   Carry at Person's Fixed Place of Business.

Again, the preliminary inquiry is, if there is carry of the weapon. If so, possession at a person's fixed place of business is especially problematic.

First, it is undeveloped by Indiana caselaw.   Second, in a business of any scale, the possessor would either have to leave the handgun at work or carry the handgun to and from work each day, which, in itself, is very risky without a license.

In most circumstances, leaving a handgun at work is a bad idea and invites problems. What if another worker obtains the gun? Where will the handgun be placed at night? Without crystal clear answers to these questions, a handgun should never be left at work. Doing so presents serious civil[97] and/or criminal risks to the possessor.

In any event, assuming that the problem of transporting to and from work can legally be resolved, many employers will not allow possession of a handgun at work.

The only logical legislative interpretation of this statutory exception is to allow the small business owner(s), or others in similar circumstances, to possess the handgun at his/her place of work. This is common, in fact, in small, high-risk businesses, such as gun stores.

This exception, moreover, harkens back to a much simpler time when most businesses were small and individually owned. However, even if the possessor owns the business, it is unlikely he/she will carry a handgun at his/her fixed place of business due to insurance restrictions and exclusions.

Finally, it is important to note that this exception only applies to a fixed place of business. If the business is conducted in multiple, varying locations, or is mobile, this exception clearly does not apply. Based on the foregoing, carrying at a person's fixed place of business, as an exception to licensing, is likely narrow in its application, and should be avoided.

[?] EXAMPLE, Mobile Dwelling and Business: *Facts:* Doris owns a motor home that cost several hundred thousand dollars. She lives in it, and conducts her business from this vehicle. She keeps her handgun in the motor home. One day, Doris is pulled over for a broken tail light. The police officer asks if she has any weapons inside, and she admits she has the handgun. She is arrested, and charged with carrying a handgun without a license. *Question:* Should she be convicted? *Answer:* Yes. There is carry and/or constructive possession. Further, motor vehicles, despite being a place of abode or business, are specifically excluded under the statutory scheme exempting licensing.[98]

VIII.   Transporting Without A License.

From the foregoing discussion, it should be apparent there must be a way to transport a handgun without a license. There is.

A.   Selected Statutory Text.

"[It is lawful for] any person [to carry] a handgun unloaded in a secure wrapper from the place of purchase to his dwelling or fixed place of business, or to a place of repair or back to his dwelling or fixed place of business, or in moving from one dwelling or business to another."[99]

B.   Scope of Right to Transport.

While the scope of exception from licensing is clear within this statute, there is an open question as to what constitutes a "secure wrapper".

C.   Standard for Secure Wrapper.

What constitutes a "secure wrapper" depends on the facts in a given situation. There is, however, a standard/test to judge this by: the handgun must be unloaded, and be situated to prevent immediate or ready access to the injurious capabilities of the weapon.[100]

The caselaw in Indiana, moreover, develops what is a "secure wrapper", often by addressing what does not meet this standard. For instance, a disassembled handgun under the vehicle seat of a possessor is not in a secure wrapper.[101]

> [†] **PRACTICAL TIP, Ensuring Secure Wrapper:** If transportation is necessary in a "secure wrapper", the weapon should be transported without ammunition, or the ammunition should be located in a separate location/container. The weapon should be completely field stripped,[102] such as for cleaning, placed in a locked box, and transported in the trunk of the vehicle, all inaccessible to the occupants. The ammunition should also be locked in a separate container and placed in the trunk.

IX.   Conclusion.

With the exception of carry on the inside of one's dwelling, or on one's real property, which would not include carry outside of one's apartment, the only other allowance for carry without a license (aside from specific legal standing exempting the requirement of licensing, such as with police powers), would be at one's fixed place of business. However, this is likely problematic, because this may necessitate transportation to and from work, which would only be legal if placed within a secure wrapper.

Any person desiring to carry a handgun with any type of frequency outside of one's dwelling is inviting unnecessary legal risk without a handgun license. This is particularly the case, given our society's very limited tolerance for those breaching security laws, post-September 11, 2001. Thus, a handgun license is always the safe and advised course of action.

Finally, it must be remembered that any possession of a gun is illegal if the possessor has a conviction for domestic battery, is a serious violent felon, or is on probation.

Chapter 2

Handgun Licensing

> One violent crime occurs in Indiana every 24.8
> minutes, breaking down to one murder every
> 24.9 hours, one forcible rape every 5.0 hours, one
> robbery every 83.7 minutes, and one aggravated
> assault every 40.9 minutes. The State has one
> property crime every 2.5 minutes, breaking down to
> one burglary every 12.8 minutes, one larceny/theft
> every 3.6 minutes, and one motor vehicle theft every
> 24.9 minutes.
> –Indiana Criminal Justice Institute, Research &
> Evaluation, Crime Trends in Indiana, Crime Clock
> 2000.

I.   Introduction.

As noted in Chapter 1, handgun possessors, unless exempted
from licensing, may only lawfully carry a handgun without a license
in limited places: in their dwelling and on their property or in their
fixed place of business.[103] Further, these exceptions have been
narrowly construed by the Courts or are undefined.[104]

Beyond these limited exceptions to licensing, the Legislature
has mandated that a person must apply for and be issued a license
in order to carry a handgun in Indiana.   This requirement certainly
affords the society at large with a measure of regulatory protection
by screening applicants to make sure they do not have obvious and
logical reasons to preclude licensing.[105]

The Legislature has effectively delegated all of the
responsibilities of handgun licensing to the Superintendent of the

Indiana State Police ("Superintendent").[106]   The Superintendent handles tasks from prescribing the form[107] for the handgun license application, which is titled Indiana Application for Handgun License (*See* Appendix "1" for a reproduction of the Indiana Application for Handgun License, which cannot be used by a reader for an actual application), to making the final decision as to whether a license shall be issued.[108]

This chapter addresses the two types of Indiana handgun permits: unlimited and qualified.   The discussion then turns to, and focuses on, the following related subject areas: (1) application;[109] (2) term,[110] renewal,[111] and replacement of a handgun license;[112] (3) name and address change;[113] (4) suspension or revocation;[114] and (5) removal of a legal disability precluding licensing.[115]

Finally, there are a substantial number of practical tips and cautions contained in this chapter that the reader is urged to follow. These should make the process of licensing easier and help lower legal risks.

II.   Selected Statutory Text.

"(a) Licenses to carry handguns shall be either qualified or unlimited. A qualified license shall be issued for hunting and target practice. . . .Unlimited licenses shall be issued for the purpose of the protection of life and property."[116]

III.   Types of Licenses.

With regard to these handgun licenses, eighty to eighty-five percent are unlimited licenses.[117] The distinction between the two licenses is effectively where a person can carry a handgun. The empowering statute, however, speaks in terms of purpose, not places to carry.

A.   Qualified License.

The use of a qualified handgun license is for hunting and target practice, but the standard effectively specifies where a person could carry: to a range to practice or the woods to hunt.[118]

[!] **CAUTION, Limits of Qualified License:**   Although this is an undeveloped area of Indiana caselaw, an applicant should always opt for the unlimited license to minimize the chance of illegally carrying. Specifically, a qualified licensee found carrying a handgun for self-defense, and clearly not target practice or hunting, could be convicted as any other unlicensed person. The qualifications for both licenses are the same. The only difference is the license fee: $5.00 for a qualified license and $15.00 for an unlimited license.[119]

B.   Unlimited License.

The unlimited license is to be used to carry a handgun for purposes of protection of life and property.[120]   With this type of handgun license, a licensee could carry a handgun throughout Indiana, subject to any other laws, rules, and regulations.

[!] **CAUTION, Limits of Unlimited License:** Despite whatever inferences might be drawn from the term "unlimited license", there are numerous and substantial civil and criminal limitations with regard to carrying a handgun with an "unlimited license". These limitations must be understood to avoid criminal and/or civil liability. Many of these limitations are discussed throughout this Book.

IV.   Application Process.

Once a person has made the personal decision to apply for a handgun license, and determined the type of license desired, qualified or unlimited, the application process is next.

A.   Where to Apply.

The point of departure with regard to the application process, is determining where to apply for and obtain an application for the license.[121] If the applicant lives in a municipality, such as a city or town, the applicant applies through the chief of police, or the top law enforcement officer of that municipality.[122]

Typically, in municipalities of any size, this top law enforcement officer will have designated officers to process the application, and have set times, places, and other policies and procedures regarding this process.[123]

If the applicant does not live in a municipality, or if there is no such municipal officer, then the applicant applies through the county sheriff's office.[124]

[†] **PRACTICAL TIP, Finding Out Where to Apply:** If the applicant is unsure where to apply for the handgun license, a telephone call to local and/or county law enforcement agencies usually will provide the answer. In towns and cities

that have expanded their boundaries over time, this may be unclear. Typically, the police agency to apply through is the agency that would respond to a 911 call. Before applying for a handgun license, or upon renewal, it is always advisable to contact the proper police agency to determine their current policies and procedures for submitting an application. Many agencies have written instruction sheets (*See* Appendix "2" for an example of such police rules for Marion County residents, which is titled "Instructions to Apply for a Personal Protection Firearms Permit Through the Indianapolis Police Department or the Marion County Sheriff's Department"). In any event, when contacting these law enforcement agencies with questions, be sure to always use the designated administrative telephone numbers, not 911 or any other emergency lines.

B.   Obtaining the Application.

Once the applicant has determined the appropriate law enforcement agency to make application, the first of two trips to that local police agency will need to take place. This first trip will be to obtain the Indiana-approved application form, along with any agency-specific instructions.[125] The applicant will take this application with him/her for completion.

C.   Completing the Application.

1.   Typing the Application.

The application is simple and uniform, and it contains most of the required statutory information needed by the Superintendent to approve or deny the application.[126]   While the application statute does not require the application be typed, many police agencies do.

Moreover, any application considered to be illegible due to poor handwriting, would be subject to denial, because the statutory criteria would not be ascertainable by the Superintendent, who makes the decision whether to issue a handgun license.[127]   Thus, for all practical purposes, the application should be typed.

> [†] **PRACTICAL TIP, Completing and Typing the Application Without Errors:** Typically, the respective law enforcement agency is not receptive to providing applicants with multiple copies of the application. Thus, typographical errors should be avoided on the first try, as the application is in carbonless triplicate. For this reason, the applicant is advised to obtain the application, make a copy of it, and fully complete the copy in long-hand, before carefully typing the original application. The hand-written version should then be destroyed.

2.   Answering Truthfully.

The application, additionally, must be answered truthfully, and failure to do so is a crime.[128] This is specifically enumerated on the face of the application, which notes as follows:

"Any person giving false information or offering false evidence to obtain a firearm license shall be deemed guilty of a felony and upon conviction may be punished by imprisonment for five (5) years to which may be added a fine of not more than $10,000."[129]

3. Notarization.

Upon completion, the applicant must then sign the completed application in the presence of a Notary Public, who will then notarize the application. Some police agencies have notaries on staff and available to applicants for a small fee, but, again, the applicant will have to check with the agency regarding this matter.

When presenting the application to the Notary Public, the applicant will have to show picture ID, such as a driver's license or passport, to prove to the Notary Public the applicant's identity.[130] If this is forgotten, it will only delay application processing and result in an additional trip.

> **[†] PRACTICAL TIP, Notarization and Completion:** The applicant will likely want to complete the notarization on the applicant's second, and final trip, to the local police agency. Thus, the applicant should call the administrative number for the law enforcement agency, to ensure the processor is actually there and a Notary Public is available. In smaller agencies, there may only be one person who handles application processing.

4. Application and License Fees.

Before returning with the completed application to the local police agency, the applicant will have to obtain two checks. The first check is to be made payable to the local police agency. This charge of $10.00 is for the local agency's processing of the application, $5.00 of which is to be refunded if the license is not issued.[131] This payment is required to be in guaranteed funds, or in some cases, cash.[132] The applicant should verify the form of payment by reviewing any instruction sheet provided with the application or by a call to the processing agency.

The second check and fee is for the license itself, and is made payable to the State of Indiana.[133] This payment cannot be made in cash or by personal check. The funds must either be paid by money order or certified check. The license fee is $5.00 for a qualified license and $15.00 for an unlimited license.[134]

V.   Submitting the Application.

Upon return to the police agency with a completed application, photo ID, and the necessary funds, the application will be finalized.

A.   Statutory Information.

The licensing statute requires the local police agency to obtain certain statutory information about the applicant to complete the application process before the application is submitted to the Superintendent. However, this is effectively the same information required on the face of the application itself.

This required statutory information is: (1) full legal name; (2) full address; (3) length of residence in the community; (4) whether the applicant's residence is located within the limits of any city or town; (5) the applicant's occupation; (6) place of business or employment; (7) criminal record, if any, and convictions (minor traffic offenses excepted); (8) age; (9) race; (10) sex; (11) nationality; (12) date of birth; (13) citizenship; (14) height; (15) weight; (16) build; (17) color of hair; (18) color of eyes; (19) scars and marks; (20) whether the applicant has previously held an Indiana license to carry a handgun and, if so, the serial number of the license and year issued; (21) whether the applicant's license has ever been suspended or revoked, and if so, the year and reason for the suspension or revocation; and (22) the applicant's reason for desiring a license.[135]

1. Minor Traffic Offenses Excepted.

The Superintendent has enacted an administrative rule to define the scope and limitations of "minor traffic offenses excepted", as enumerated in item "(7)".

Specifically, the minor traffic offenses that must be included on the application, and that are not excluded under item "(7)", are as follows: (1) driving under the influence of alcohol, drugs, or narcotics; (2) reckless driving; (3) fleeing a police officer; and (4) any charges relating to injury or death.[136]

All other minor traffic offenses, such as a speeding ticket, are excluded from the disclosure requirement on the application.

B. Local Agency Processing.

Typically, on this second trip to the local police agency, the application will be reviewed by the police agency to make sure it is complete. This fulfills the police official's requirement to obtain the requisite statutory information.[137] Then the applicant will be finger-printed.[138] This is a full battery of fingerprints and is a messy process.

The local police agency will then internally process the application and is required to conduct its own investigation.[139] By statute, the processing officer or police agency can inquire into the applicant's official records,[140] verify the accuracy of the information on the application, and verify the applicant's character and reputation by a records inquiry.[141]

The police agency then will make a recommendation to the Superintendent to approve or deny the application,[142] and mail it to the Superintendent.

VI.   Approval or Denial of Application.

A.   Time for Processing.

By statute, the Superintendent has sixty days from the time the application is filed to deny or approve the application. Upon receipt of the application by the Superintendent, the Superintendent's processor may make any further investigation deemed necessary regarding the applicant.[143]

If denial of the application has been recommended by the local police agency, the Superintendent must be provided written, complete, and specific reasons for this negative recommendation.[144]

The Superintendent will consider this recommendation in determining whether the applicant is a "proper person" and has a "proper reason", which is the standard on which a license shall issue and the reason for all of the requested information about the applicant.

B.   Shall-Issue Requirement.

Because Indiana is a shall-issue state,[145] there is no discretion for the Superintendent, upon investigation, to deny an application that conforms to the statutory and administrative criteria. Thus, if the

Superintendent considers this information and finds that the applicant is a "proper person" and has a "proper reason", the license must be issued.

C. Proper Person.

A "proper person" is firstly defined under a lengthy description in the statutory section of the article on weapons. The definition, specifically, is in the negative in what the applicant does not have in his/her background.

1. Statutory Definition.

A "proper person" is a person who does not have any of the following: (1) a conviction for resisting law enforcement within five years before the person applies for license; (2) a conviction for a crime for which he/she could have been sentenced for more than one year; (3) a record of being an alcohol or drug abuser as defined in the licensing scheme; (4) documented evidence that would give rise to a reasonable belief that he/she has a propensity for violent or emotionally unstable conduct; (5) any false statement of material fact on his/her application; (6) a conviction for any crime involving an inability to safely handle a handgun; (7) a conviction for violation of the provisions of Article 47 of the criminal code (the criminal code for weapons and instruments of violence); or (8) an adjudication as a delinquent child for an act that would be a felony if committed by an adult, if the person applying for a license or permit is less than twenty-three years of age.[146]

2. Re-Codification.

In 2001, the Legislature re-codified the application statute, adding additional qualifications that, effectively, broaden the requirements of a "proper person".

This re-codification did not repeal the "proper person" statute, so both are applicable to the Superintendent's determination of whether to issue a license based on the applicant being a "proper person". However, there are overlaps between certain disqualifiers.

Under this statutory re-codification, the Superintendent shall not issue a license to carry a handgun (again defined in the negative) to any person who: (1) has been convicted of a felony; (2) is under eighteen years of age; (3) is under twenty-three years of age, if the person has been adjudicated a delinquent child for an act that would be a felony if committed by an adult; or (4) has been arrested for a Class A or Class B felony, or any other felony that was committed while armed with a deadly weapon, or that involved the use of violence, if a court has found probable cause to believe that the person committed the offense, although a license may be issued to a person who was acquitted of the specific offense or if the charges were dismissed.[147]

3.   Administrative Rule.

In addition to the foregoing, the Superintendent has enacted a set of administrative rules that may make an applicant an "improper person" and not subject to licensing, in certain circumstances.

First, an applicant is an "improper person" if issuance of the handgun license would place the licensee in contradiction of any federal firearms law.

Secondly, an applicant is an "improper person" if he/she has a history of minor criminal activity that would give rise to a reasonable belief that he/she has a propensity for violent or emotionally unstable conduct.

Thirdly, the applicant is an "improper person" if he/she is found, upon a standard of reasonable belief, not to be emotionally stable.[148]

4. Written Recommendations.

The Superintendent may also receive written, specific recommendations for disapproval by a local police agency or sheriff's department. The local agency's recommendation may only be followed by the Superintendent if the applicant, by virtue of the information provided in the written recommendations, is not, in fact, a "proper person" or the applicant does not have a "proper reason".

D. Proper Reason.

A "proper reason" is defined to be for the defense of oneself or the State.[149] If the applicant is found to be a "proper person" and have a "proper reason", the license shall be issued.

E. Denial.

If denied a license, the applicant is entitled to an administrative hearing before an administrative law judge. To be successful at such a hearing, the applicant would have to establish that he/she is, in fact, a "proper person" and has a "proper reason". In all reality, this will require the assistance of legal counsel.

VII.   Term, Renewal, and Replacement.

A.   Term.

From the date of issuance of either a qualified or unlimited license, the license is valid for a period of four years, unless suspended or revoked.[150]

The form of the Indiana handgun license clearly indicates the "issued" and "expires" date on the face of the license itself (*See* Appendix "3" for an example of an Indiana License to Carry Handgun). As such, this matter should not lead to confusion or require computation of time by the licensee.   If a licensee uses a computerized calendar, this expiration date (and a renewal reminder) should be immediately entered on the licensee's calendar program so the license does not inadvertently expire.

B.   Renewal.

With respect to renewal of the handgun license, the licensee could, obviously, face a situation where the license would expire before a renewal application is decided upon by the Superintendent. The statutory scheme for licensing resolves this dilemma. It provides that any renewal application, filed within thirty days of expiration of the license, automatically extends the validity of the existing license until determination of renewal.[151]

C.   Replacement.

Finally, if a handgun permit is lost or damaged, a replacement may be obtained for a $5.00 fee. Given the power inherent in a license and growing concerns about identity theft, the licensee should take great care to avoid losing his/her license.[152]

VIII.   Name or Address Change.

Consistent with the higher level of security post-September 11, 2001, the application provision of the licensing statutory scheme has changed.[153] The most notable, and common sense change, is the requirement that a licensee notify the Superintendent of any changes of his/her name or address within sixty days of the change(s).[154]

This notification requirement specifies no particular remedy for failure to comply, but other law indicates this is likely a Class B misdemeanor.[155]   Furthermore, if the failure was an attempt to circumvent the licensing requirements, the licensee would commit a felony on renewal, by giving false information on his/her application. Finally, and perhaps most importantly, any notices, such as suspensions issued, would be sent to an incorrect person and/or address.

IX.   Suspension or Revocation.

By statute[156] and administrative rule,[157] the Superintendent may suspend/revoke an issued license based on reasonable grounds.

A.   Statutory Immediate Suspension.

Specifically, documented evidence that a licensee is not now a "proper person" for a license constitutes grounds for immediate suspension or revocation of a previously issued handgun license.[158] The permit holder is formally notified by a suspension letter. (*See* Appendix "4" for an example of an actual Letter of Suspension).

37

B.   Administrative Temporary Suspension.

The statutory scheme for suspension and revocation further authorizes the Superintendent to enact administrative rules and regulations concerning the procedures for suspending or revoking a person's license.[159]

The Superintendent has enacted such administrative rules and regulations.[160] The central administrative rule allows temporary suspension of a license upon the written request of a local police department, sheriff's department, prosecutor, or full time police officer, without a prior hearing.[161]

However, the Superintendent will only suspend a person's permit if reasonable grounds are given in the request.[162] The suspended licensee would be given an immediate hearing on the suspension.[163] At this hearing, the person or entity that requested the suspension must appear and prove grounds for permanent revocation of the license.[164] Failure of this person or entity to appear at the hearing may cause reinstatement.[165]

The Superintendent will only permanently revoke a license under statutory or administrative rules if he has proof of the allegation that provides the grounds for a temporary suspension.[166] Further, the licensee is entitled to an administrative hearing on such a permanent revocation.[167] Even a revocation may be vacated under the right circumstances.[168] (*See* Appendix "5" for a Letter of Reinstatement).

X.   Removal of Disability.

It is possible that a disability causing an applicant not to be a "proper person" can be removed through a variety of means.

The most likely mechanism for removal of a disability that would otherwise prevent the issuance of a license by the Superintendent, is a full pardon by the Governor of Indiana. A full pardon will remove the barriers to licensing presented by most felonies, or any violations of the handgun licensing statute, if the pardon removes the disability causing the applicant not to be a "proper person". However, fifteen years must have elapsed between the time of the offense and the application for a handgun license.

A conditional pardon for a felony, or for a violation of the handgun license chapter, may remove a disability to reinstate the person's status as a "proper person". However, this is only the case if the Superintendent, after investigation, determines that the circumstances have changed since the pardoned conviction to such an extent that the pardoned person is now likely to handle handguns in compliance with the law.[169]

XI.   Conclusion.

Without question, the disqualifiers to being a "proper person" are complex, as are the statutes and administrative rules encompassing suspension and/or revocation of a license. That stated, the typical applicant will not be involved with these issues.

Given the Superintendent's carefully constructed application, the actual application process is simple and relatively easy. The overall time commitment required is minimal. Thus, in all circumstances, any person involved with handguns should apply for and obtain an unlimited license.

Chapter 3

Handgun License Reciprocity

> Reciprocal laws: "Laws of one state which extend rights and privileges to citizens of another state if such state grants similar privileges to citizens of the first state."
> –*Black's Law Dictionary* 1269 (7th ed. 1999)

I.   Introduction.

Perhaps one of the most misunderstood matters facing any licensee is state-to-state reciprocity. Indiana has a reciprocity statute that allows foreign permit holders to carry a handgun in Indiana.[170] Indiana's handgun permits, likewise, are recognized by certain other states to allow for lawful carry of a handgun in that reciprocal state.[171]

This area of handgun law is consistently expressed to the author to be of great interest to licensees. However, due to the lack of federal preemption, this is a very complex area of law.

The most important concept for the licensee to grasp is that carry in a reciprocal state is only in accordance with the laws of the reciprocal state. Thus, an Indiana licensee carrying in Florida, under Florida's reciprocity statute, would be bound in all terms of carry by Florida law and any applicable federal law.

Thus, if the licensee desires to carry his/her handgun in another state, a complete understanding of the laws of the reciprocal state can mean the difference, literally, between no problem with the foreign carry of the handgun, on the one hand, to arrest, conviction, and imprisonment, on the other.

II.   Preemption.

As noted, the reciprocal licensing schemes are state,[172] and not federal, in nature. What is the significance of this?

A.   Federal.

Under the U.S. Constitution's Commerce and Supremacy Clauses, the Congress could preempt this area as a matter of interstate commerce, and enact a uniform national carry statutory scheme.[173] This would largely avoid the licensee from having to understand the firearms laws of the reciprocal states of carry. Federal law would govern and control. This is not the case.

While a federal carry license has long been advocated, at least with respect to police officers, the proposed federal standard has failed to come to fruition.[174] Thus, without state-level statutory reciprocity, there would be no interstate carrying of any handgun by a licensee in a foreign state.

B.   State.

The preemption doctrine also must be understood and considered on the state level. If a given state's legislature has "preempted" the field, then only it can pass gun laws in the state. This, therefore, precludes local governmental units (towns, cities, counties, and the like) from enacting a patchwork of local laws.

In any state without state-level preemption of firearms laws, the licensee must exercise extreme caution in reciprocal carry, as the handgun laws may change from one municipality to another within a given state.

The Indiana Legislature has effectively preempted lawmaking regarding firearms by local governmental units.[175]

III.   Selected Statutory Text.

"(b) Licenses to carry handguns, issued by other states or foreign countries, will be recognized according to the terms thereof but only while the holders are not residents of Indiana."[176]

IV.   Carry Protocol.

The licensee contemplating reciprocal interstate carry should engage in three steps to evaluate the propriety of such carry: (1) determine reciprocity; (2) investigate the laws of the reciprocal state; and (3) determine the propriety of carry under a cost/benefit analysis.

A.   Determine Reciprocity.

The threshold question in contemplating interstate carry is to determine if the foreign jurisdiction is a reciprocal state: Does state X recognize and afford authority to an Indiana license?

Researching reciprocal states and their laws is quite difficult and complex.   There is no room for an error of law, as the permit holder will be in a foreign place, and far from home.

A list is provided below of the states that clearly recognize an Indiana license as of January 1, 2004.   Additional sources of information regarding reciprocity are the National Rifle Association and the attorney general and/or secretary of state of the respective jurisdictions, which usually have printed and/or on-line research materials available to the licensee.

Finally, even if another state appears to be a reciprocal state, a permit holder must remember one maxim: The firearms laws of the several states are constantly in flux and are often inconsistent, and each state may have its own unique assortment of state and local laws, rules, regulations, practices, and customs, all in addition to federal laws.

B. Investigate Foreign Laws.

If reciprocity exists, the key for lawful carry in a reciprocal state is for the Indiana licensee to research the reciprocal laws well in advance of interstate travel. This research must be updated to the last minute of interstate travel to ensure accuracy.

1. Travel Boundaries and State Preemption.

To properly research reciprocal laws, the licensee must determine, to the extent possible, his/her travel boundaries. This is particularly the case in a state without state-level preemption, as there may be a wide variance of local laws respecting firearms.

2. Review Resource Materials.

With reciprocity, travel boundaries, and preemption determined, any and all published state-specific guides[177] and/or the information available from the reciprocal state's attorney general, secretary of state, and/or state police, must be reviewed. This is to ensure a working knowledge of the relevant law.

3. Clarify Ambiguous Issues.

Ideally, any remaining unclear or grey areas of carry to the licensee of the reciprocal state's laws should be discussed with a knowledgeable person in the particular reciprocal state, such as an attorney.

C. Cost/Benefit Analysis.

Every act of carrying a handgun involves a cost/benefit analysis, which many licensees do not fully understand. For instance, the mere act of carrying a handgun involves a specific cost/benefit analysis and determination: Is the risk of an unjustified use of force outweighed by the proper use of self-defense?

This analysis applies to carry in another state. Specifically, if the reason for interstate reciprocal carry is not significant, or the reciprocal state law is not clearly understood by the licensee, then this should give the licensee great pause to the contemplated carry. Simply put, is the benefit of interstate carry more important than the risks associated with carry?

V. Major Legal Differences Between the States.

State-to-state limitations and restrictions on carry widely vary. In fact, if the reciprocal state gun laws are not preempted on a state level, there may be a wide array of variance in the laws even within that state. There are, however, several common areas of regulation among other states that are different from or not found in Indiana:

- Churches
- Major Events
- Bars/Taverns (places where alcohol is served)
- Police Encounters (legal duty to tell the officer)
- Private Property
- State/Local Government Property (leased or owned)
- Political Meetings
- Financial Institutions
- Courthouses/Courtrooms
- Concealed Carry (concealed or open carry required)

VI.   Reciprocal States.

Presently, an Indiana unlimited license is recognized only in the following states:

- Alabama[178]
- Alaska[179]
- Colorado[180]
- Florida[181]
- Georgia[182]
- Idaho[183]
- Kentucky[184]
- Michigan[185]
- Montana[186]
- New Hampshire[187]
- Oklahoma[188]
- South Dakota[189]
- Tennessee[190]
- Utah[191]
- Vermont[192]
- Wyoming[193]

VII.   Conclusion.

Reciprocal carry is extremely complex.   However, with careful research and planning, lawful reciprocal carry can be effectuated.   Take nothing for granted and make no assumptions. Finally, given that the Indiana license itself affords reciprocity, most reciprocal states require physical possession of the Indiana license and picture identification for lawful carry.

48

PART II:
LIMITS ON HANDGUN CARRY

> "The essence of a free government consists in an
> effectual control of rivalries."
> –John Adams, *Discourses on Davila* (1789)

It is the author's opinion that many, if not most, licensees believe they can carry a handgun throughout Indiana without restriction. This is simply not the case.[194]

Most fundamentally, there are significant Indiana and federal statutory, criminal limitations on the right to carry a handgun with a license.[195] In order to avoid serious legal consequences, including arrest, prosecution, and felony conviction, a licensee must fully understand the limits of the rights of his/her license.

A useful model to assist in understanding the limits on carrying of a handgun with a permit, is to think of an Indiana-issued handgun license like an Indiana motor vehicle operator's license.

The driver's license broadly authorizes a licensed driver to operate a motor vehicle throughout Indiana, just as the handgun permit authorizes the carry of a handgun throughout Indiana.[196] Other Indiana and federal authority (including statutes, rules, regulations, caselaw interpretations, and court orders), then place substantial limitations on this right.[197]

[?] EXAMPLE, Comparison of Handgun Permit Rights with Driver's License Authority: The right to operate a motor vehicle is limited by criminal law. For example, a driver is prohibited from operating while intoxicated or speeding in a school zone. A handgun licensee, likewise, cannot brandish a handgun[198] or carry a handgun on school grounds.[199]

What follows in Part II is an enumeration and analysis of the Indiana and federal limits on the carry of a handgun with a license. There are five general categories of limitation: (1) Indiana statutory restrictions;[200] (2) administrative and regulatory restrictions;[201] (3) courthouse restrictions;[202] (4) federal restrictions,[203] and (5) private property restrictions.[204]

I.   Indiana Statutory Restrictions.

Chapter 4 considers the exception to licensed carry related to Indiana penal and juvenile facilities. The penal statute makes no exception for licensees. The most problematic issue for the licensee regarding this exception is being able to identify the non-traditional prison-type facilities, which may not have any of the traditional indicia of a jail: fences, guard towers, razor wire, walls, and bars.

Chapter 5 addresses the most broad and risky exception for licensees: schools. With the narrow exception of a licensee dropping off or picking up a person from a school, handguns are prohibited on school property, on school buses, and at school functions. The definition of a school is broad and lacks clearly defined boundaries.

The final Indiana statutory restriction is analyzed in Chapter 6 and is likely the most familiar. This is the preclusion of guns in controlled areas of airports and on commercial and charter flights. There are no exceptions for the licensee for carry in these areas.

II.   Indiana Administrative Restrictions.

At both the Indiana and federal level, administrative agencies have adopted administrative rules concerning firearms. These laws preclude handguns in certain areas, and subject a licensee to expulsion from the venue and confiscation of the weapon, but may not necessarily afford criminal liability. These restrictions apply to the annual state fair (Chapter 7), riverboat casinos (Chapter 8), and maritime ports (Chapter 9). None of these administrative rules except licensees.

III.   Courthouse and/or Courtroom Restrictions.

Chapter 10 covers the confusing and misunderstood area of firearms in courthouses. In short, despite having a license, a handgun cannot be carried into Indiana courthouses and/or courtrooms.

IV.   Federal Restrictions.

With the exception of lawful hunting on federal land, any federal property that has regularly employed federal personnel present, prohibits the possession of any firearm on the premises. No Indiana licenses are recognized. This is addressed in Chapter 11. There is also overlap of such preclusions by federal rules and regulations, but because the preclusion for federal property is clear by statute, these overlapping regulations are not included in this discussion, although a select example is provided.

Finally, Chapter 12 addresses the preclusion of carrying weapons on mass transportation. This is a developing and relatively confused area of the law, affected by overlapping state laws, administrative rules and regulations, and private carrier policies.

V.   Private Property Restrictions.

Chapter 13 explores the last major area of restriction regarding carrying a handgun: those restrictions that arise from the right of real property interest holders to regulate affairs on their own property, which may include firearms restrictions. These private restrictions supersede the rights of a licensee while on such property.

A final qualification, while the author intends this listing to be complete on major limitation areas, laws are fluid and constantly changing. In fact, drastic changes may occur over a very short period of time. Thus, new or revised limits may exist, and any specific questions should be directed to an individual's legal counsel.

Chapter 4

Penal and Juvenile Facilities

> In 2002, state and federal prison authorities had under their jurisdiction 1,400,655 inmates, with 1,277,127 under state jurisdiction and 163,528 under federal jurisdiction.
> –U.S. Department of Justice, Office of Justice Programs, Bureau of Justice Statistics, Corrections Statistics for 2002

I.   Introduction.

Anyone who has ever entered a penal facility,[205] understands their stark reality. These facilities warehouse deviants for rehabilitation[206] and many dangerous[207] members of our society. As such, there is a corresponding need for rigid, but fair and humane, control in these facilities.[208]

It is understandable, therefore, that the jailers are not allowed to have guns in secure areas of prisons.[209] Nor is it surprising that the Legislature has enacted a statute that makes it a criminal offense for the populus at large to carry a deadly weapon into jail-type facilities.[210]

There are no statutory exceptions for Indiana licensees.[211] Thus, a handgun cannot be lawfully carried into any penal or juvenile facilities.

II.   Selected Statutory Text.

". . .A person who . . .knowingly or intentionally: (1) delivers, or carries into the penal facility or juvenile facility with the intent to deliver, an article [of contraband] to an inmate or child of the facility… commits trafficking with an inmate. . . ."[212]

III.   Crime and Punishment.

A.   Crime.

A licensee found carrying a handgun into a jail facility would be subject to arrest, prosecution, and conviction for trafficking with an inmate.[213]   Furthermore, because the contraband in question is a handgun, which is classified as a deadly weapon,[214]   the crime of trafficking is enhanced from a Class A misdemeanor to a C felony.[215]

B.   Burden of Proof.

As with all truly[216] criminal acts, the prosecution has the burden to prove all of the elements of the crime beyond a reasonable doubt.[217]

C.   Defenses.

If the prosecution meets its burden, the defendant has the burden of proof on any affirmative defense.[218] There are several potential defenses as follows:

1.   Traditional Facilities.

If the licensee "forgot" he/she had a handgun and "accidently" carried the handgun into a traditional detention-type facility, he/she could have a general defense to the crime. An element of the crime itself, requires the handgun be "intentionally or knowingly" (technically known as the *mens rea* or "intent" element of the crime) carried into the facility, with the intent being focused, additionally, on delivery to an inmate or child.[219]

A jury determines the validity of this defense, which would, in all probability, fail. Specifically, the author believes that a violation of such criminal law at a traditional-type penal facility, would allow knowledge to be inferred and a conviction to stand, given the foregoing.

This is particularly the case because there is normally signage indicating that weapons are prohibited at jail facilities.[220] Furthermore, the metal detectors and other environmental factors would be a further mental reminder. Certainly, the prosecution would argue this, all to bolster their position that these facts create an inference supporting the intent element of the crime.[221]

Even if this defense was ultimately successful, it would be only after the licensee was arrested, booked, prosecuted, forfeited the handgun, and incurred thousands of dollars in criminal defense fees. To be clear, the responsible licensee should never find himself/herself in this situation, as this defense would likely fail.

2. Non-Traditional Facilities.

The *mens rea* element of the crime for a defense is more likely to be successfully applied to non-traditional adult and juvenile facilities. Specifically, there are a vast array of non-traditional facilities, which do not in any way mirror a traditional jail facility (no visible guards, fences, towers, bars, and the like); they may be nothing more than private residences. In such cases, it is possible that a careless licensee would "stumble" into such a facility.[222] Thus, the defense for lack of requisite intent may be successful in this type of case.

3. Non-Controlled Areas.

One general and/or affirmative defense that is apparent from the statutory language, would be if the licensee possessed his/her handgun, but properly stowed it on facility property in a non-controlled area. A classic example would be if the weapon was properly stowed and locked in the licensee's vehicle in the facility parking lot. However, the parking lot may even be considered to be a controlled area. This is not well developed in Indiana, and should not be relied upon without further investigation (as noted below).

4. Approval by Institution.

There is a provision to allow, with prior written approval, a weapon to be taken into the facility for proper purposes. Thus, even though the elements of the crime were met, this affirmative defense would excuse the act. It is not envisioned that this exception would generally apply to a licensee. It is likely applied to a weapon manufacturer's representative, who would be taking samples to a prison for inspection by personnel.[223]

D. Punishment.

A Class C felony carries a presumptive sentence of four years in prison, with aggravating circumstances allowing up to an additional four years or mitigating circumstances subtracting up to two years, from the presumptive sentence.[224]

IV. What Constitutes Adult or Juvenile Facility.

The statutory preclusion for trafficking with an inmate in contraband in a penal facility, in its most basic form, has been on the books for years.[225] It is focused on adults in traditional jail-type facilities. Such facilities should easily be identified by the licensee.

The statute also encompasses a variety of non-traditional adult facilities as well. The trafficking statute, moreover, has recently been amended and expanded to encompass a wide variety of juvenile facilities.[226]

> **[!] CAUTION, Appearance Does Not Control Scope of Preclusion:** The reader is strongly cautioned that many facilities included in this carry ban, are not stereotypical jails, prisons, and institutions that might occur to a licensee: those with fences, towers, guards, and bars. Such facilities may be simple homes or buildings in cities, towns and residential areas.

These non-traditional type of facilities encompassed within this preclusion must be recognized to avoid legal peril and violation of the law by a licensee carrying his/her handgun into a controlled area.

A.   Adult Penal Facilities.

An adult "penal facility," is broadly defined to encompass any place holding a person under a sentence, awaiting trial, or tried and convicted and awaiting sentencing for a criminal offense.[227] It includes, but is not limited to, an Indiana prison, correctional facility, county jail, penitentiary, house of correction, or other such facility.[228] Finally, it includes any correctional facilities constructed under the Indiana Office Building Commission, which may include mental health facilities.[229]

57

[?] EXAMPLE, Halfway House is Penal Facility: *Facts:* Donnie is visiting his friend at a private halfway house. He is arrested while there because he is found carrying his handgun, although he has a valid permit. Without objection or defense to the intent to deliver, the prosecution establishes the elements of the crime. Donnie's sole defense is that the halfway house is not a penal facility. *Question:* Should Donnie's conviction stand? *Answer:* Yes, because the halfway house is under contract by the Indiana Department of Corrections, and falls within the "any other facility for confinement of persons under sentence" provision.

B.   Juvenile Facilities.

As noted, the trafficking statute has been amended to include juvenile facilities. These facilities are of two types: (1) secure facilities, and (2) shelter care facilities.[230]

The children placed in these facilities are juvenile delinquents, or those in need of state-provided and monitored services by virtue of abuse or neglect, all while awaiting adjudication or adjudicated. Typically, secure facilities hold the dangerous juvenile delinquents.

1.   Secure Facility.

The first type of juvenile facility is a "secure facility". This is a place of residence, other than a shelter care facility, where a child is detained and prohibited from leaving.[231]

The purpose of this type of facility is apparent, as is the preclusion from carrying a handgun with a license. Specifically, unless a juvenile is waived to and tried as an adult in the court, a child is treated not as a criminal *per se*, but a "delinquent" due to age. However, the delinquent's acts are typically those that are criminal in nature for adults, and hence the corresponding need arises to have the juvenile physically detained.

2. Shelter Care Facility.

Secondly, a juvenile facility may be even a less formal, "shelter care facility", and may merely be a place of residence for a juvenile that is licensed but not "locked" in any fashion, unless locking is determined necessary to protect a child's health.[232]

These juvenile facilities typically house non-delinquents who are the product of neglect or abuse (CHINS kids). All such juvenile facilities preclude the carrying of a handgun, even with an Indiana license.

V. Federal Prisons.

The federal prison[233] correction system has a comparable statute regarding the carrying of firearms[234] into federal prisons with the intent to deliver to an inmate.[235] A person found in violation of this statute would be prosecuted. Conviction subjects the defendant to a fine and imprisonment for up to ten years.[236]

As will be noted in the discussion of federal property in Chapter 11, a license is generally not recognized under federal jurisdiction and, as such, a licensee cannot, as a general rule, enter onto any federal grounds with firearms. Thus, there is no lawful ability to even park at a federal prison and leave the weapon in a vehicle, if the parking lot is on federal property.

VI.   Carry Protocol.

Firearms may not be possessed at any place on federal property with a correctional facility, and must be properly stowed in advance.

With careful planning, any licensee faced with carry of his/her weapon around and/or in an Indiana adult penal or juvenile facility, can lawfully address the matter. Because carrying a handgun with a license is a substantial responsibility, proper and lawful carry always requires thought and planning on an advanced and on-going basis.

Conceptually, the licensee should consider the activities for his/her day. If any location could fit within the noted adult penal or juvenile facility preclusion, the matter must be specifically addressed and a decision made about what to do with the handgun.

To lawfully address such matters, specifically, the licensee must successfully answer three questions to continue with carry:

1.   Is such a facility encompassed in the prohibition?

2.   If so, what constitutes the facility's outer boundaries under the criminal trafficking act. Is this the parking lot? The reception area?

3.   How can the weapon be properly secured prior to entering any controlled area?

[!] CAUTION, Securing of Weapon While in Penal Facility: Whenever the weapon is to be left while visiting a penal facility, it must be secured. This would not merely constitute being left in one's vehicle, even if this would comply with the penal institution's requirements. A vehicle gun safe or trunk storage is minimally required.

Typically, the licensee will have one of three choices regarding the handgun and proper stowage when entering a controlled area of an adult penal or juvenile facility.

A. Stowage of Weapon at Home.

In any circumstance, if a licensee intends to visit an adult penal facility or juvenile facility, the safe, and always preferred course of action, is to leave the handgun properly stowed at home.

This is because an error of judgment in whether the facility is an adult penal or juvenile facility may be made. Also, an error may be made as to controlled areas where the preclusion applies. Finally, having a gun near such a facility is inviting, at best, detainment.

B. Securing Handgun in Vehicle.

In walk-in type facilities, such as local police stations and county jails, the handgun may be able to remain locked in the vehicle in public parking areas. However, any control point related to the facility, would clearly be within the prohibited zone. This may include the parking lot.

C.   Checking Weapon.

Virtually all facilities have gun-check lockers, which may be available to the civilian licensee, with more latitude and courtesy typically being given to those with more or less official business, such as attorneys or clergy.

Do not enter a police station, jail, city building or similar facility with a handgun. This is inviting detainment.

A telephone call to the facility is a simple and proper way to answer this question, and other questions the licensee may have. It is always the licensee's responsibility to take steps to avoid legal peril.

> [†] **PRACTICAL TIP, Call Facility:** A call should be placed to any jail-type facility in every instance where there is a question in the permit holder's view, in order to ensure compliance with the law. In some facilities, such as large Indiana or federal prisons, the parking lot may be a controlled space. Thus, merely possessing a handgun in one's vehicle could constitute a crime. In the case of a juvenile facility, the fact that the facility falls within this preclusion may not be apparent without a call or further inquiry.

Even if a gun-check locker is available, this method will be disfavored by most all facilities. Use of lockers is rife with liability issues, and labor intensive for such facilities, especially in this time of tight budgetary constraints.

VII.   Conclusion.

Carrying a concealed handgun into any type of Indiana

penal facility, adult or juvenile, is prohibited. There is no exception for a lawfully possessed handgun by a licensee. Being found with a handgun, could subject the licensee to arrest, prosecution, and conviction for trafficking with an inmate.

The licensee must also be aware that there are non-traditional, and perhaps even hard to identify, adult and juvenile facilities. Thus, the licensee must always be cognizant of his/her carry.

There is a potential defense if the licensee truly did not remember he/she had possession of the weapon in the facility or was unaware of the facility. However, a responsible licensee should never be in this situation. When visiting a jail facility, the licensee must stow his/her weapon in a fully secured place, such as a gun safe.

Finally, no firearms are allowed on federal prison property. An Indiana license is not recognized in any way under federal law.

Chapter 5

Schools, Buses, and Functions

> For the 2002-03 school year, Indiana had 1,001,937 students enrolled in public schools.
> –Indiana Department of Education, Indiana Education Statistics, Trend Graphs
>
> "Kindergartners carried knife, pistol onto bus"
> –Front Page Headline Indianapolis Star, March 5, 2004

I.   Introduction.

The problem of firearms in schools was crystallized by the tragic events that occurred in Columbine, Colorado, on April 21, 1999. This galvanized the Nation to act in preventing school violence and shootings from occurring again.[237] Unfortunately, juveniles with weapons at schools still remains problematic.

It is not surprising that the Legislature long ago enacted a sweeping statutory scheme that criminalizes the possession of firearms[238] at schools.[239] This firearm[240] prohibition includes handguns[241] carried/possessed by licensees.[242]

A licensee cannot carry a handgun in, or on, school property, on property being used for a school function, or on a school bus. This statute creates a grave risk for licensees, and it is imperative for the licensee to understand its potentially broad and undefined scope.

There is a similar restriction precluding possession of a firearm in a school zone as a matter of federal law.[243]

II.   Selected Statutory Text.

"A person who possesses a firearm: (1) in or on school property; (2) in or on property that is being used by a school for a school function; or (3) on a school bus; commits a Class D felony."[243]

"This chapter [prohibiting guns at schools] . . . does not apply to. . . .(3) A person who (A) may legally possess a firearm; and (B) possesses the firearm in a motor vehicle that is being operated by the person to transport another person to or from a school or a school function."[245]

III.   Crime and Punishment.

A.   Crime.

Any individual not excluded by the statute,[246] who possesses a firearm in a school, on school property, on a school bus, or at a school function, including a licensee, is subject to arrest, prosecution, and conviction of a Class D felony.[247]

B.   Burden of Proof.

The prosecution has the burden to prove, beyond a reasonable doubt, that the defendant possessed a gun in or on school property, at a school function, or on a school bus.[248]

C.   Defenses.

1.   Strict Liability.

This criminal statute has no provision for a defense based on a lack of intent. It appears to create strict criminal liability.[249]

2.   Affirmative Defense.

The statute does contain one affirmative defense[250] that may readily apply to licensees.[251] Specifically, it allows the licensee to possess a handgun in his/her vehicle while transporting another person to or from school or a school function.[252]

> **[?] EXAMPLE, Indiana Case, Defining an Affirmative Defense to Carry on School Property:** The Indiana Court of Appeals defined this affirmative defense in its 2003 *Newson* case. This appellate court held that this statutory language created an affirmative defense, but strictly applied this defense and affirmed the defendant's conviction. This was because even though the defendant lawfully possessed the handgun and a license, his vehicle was parked at a loading dock (with his handgun therein) while he was inside the school building. Therefore, he was not "operating" the vehicle and the affirmative defense was not applicable.[253]

D.   Punishment.

A Class D felony has a presumptive sentence of one and one-half years in prison, subject to aggravation of the sentence up by the same amount of time, or three years total, or mitigation downward from the presumptive sentence, by one year.[254]

IV.   What Constitutes School Property.

The term "school property" is not defined within the particular chapter of the applicable criminal statute.[255] However, the term is defined in other statutory provisions[256] that apply to the entire penal code.[257] The caselaw also clearly provides that this definition of "school property" applies to the guns-on-school-property crime.[258]

The definition of "school property" is complex because it references several other statutes. Such "school property," includes, but is not necessarily limited to, buildings and land used by: (1) school corporations;[259] (2) licensed residential child care establishments, including group and foster homes;[260] (3) licensed day care facilities, including child care centers, child care homes, and child care ministries;[261] (4) private schools;[262] and (5) all federal, state, local, or nonprofit programs or services operated to serve, assist, or otherwise benefit children who are at least three years of age, but not yet enrolled in kindergarten; this includes, but is not limited to, Head Start, a special education preschool program, or a developmental child care program for preschool children.[263]

This definition of "school property" also includes the grounds adjacent to, and owned or rented, in common with the school building or structure.[264]

This broad definition of "school property" is problematic for licensees and its outer boundaries are not well defined. Further, because the crime is one of apparent strict liability, a simple failure to understand what constitutes school property, does not create a criminal defense.

[?] **EXAMPLE, Indiana Case, Demonstrating Breadth of School Property:** The Indiana Supreme Court's 2002 *French* decision highlights the fact that the definition of "school property" is liberally and broadly construed. In this case, the defendant's crime was enhanced for dealing drugs within 1000 feet of "school property." The "school property" was a church that operated a quasi-kindergarten. Thus, it would appear that a licensed parishioner, carrying a handgun to Sunday church, would be subject to arrest, and conviction, if the church had even an informal type of school,[265] and many churches do have such operations.

What exactly constitutes "school property" is, as noted, unanswered in Indiana, but the *French* opinion directs that this will be broadly defined. Likely, when, and if, a case finally pinpoints this definition, it will be broad, as in *French*, and will likely track a broad dictionary-type definition.

> **[?] EXAMPLE, School Field Trip:** *Facts:* Sara is accompanying her daughter on a field trip. She arrives at the school, parks, locks her gun in her auto safe, and then enters the school and goes on the field trip. She is licensed to carry a handgun. Sara gets into a discussion with another parent about self-defense, and mentions how her gun is stored in her car. This parent uses her cell phone to alert the police. Upon return to the school, Sara is arrested. *Question:* Should Sara be convicted? *Answer:* Yes, because under the foregoing statutory analysis, a licensee cannot drive to the school, leave the handgun in his/her parked vehicle on school property, and thereafter attend a school field trip.[266]

The substantial unanswered question is if the statutory prohibition of guns at schools applies to post-secondary education.[267] Unless and until this is clarified in the law, the only prudent assumption is that this statutory prohibition also applies to colleges, trade schools, and the like.[268]

V.   What Constitutes a School Bus.

Within the applicable criminal and/or educational statutes, two types of school buses are defined. The first is the standard school bus, and is classified as a motor vehicle that is designed and constructed to carry ten or more Indiana school children.[269]

The second is the special purpose bus, which is any motor vehicle that is designed and constructed to carry six passengers, and used by a school corporation for transportation purposes not appropriate for school buses.[270]

This is a relatively simple definition, and applied against narrow allowance for the possession while transporting a person to a school or school function, clearly directs no licensee may possess a handgun on a "school bus" and/or "special purpose bus" at any time, such as on a chaperoned school field trip.

VI.   What Constitutes a School Function.

What constitutes a "school function" is equally problematic. Unfortunately, there are no general enumerations of school functions available. Furthermore, the limits on a "school function" cannot be determined with any precision because the term is not defined by statute or interpretational caselaw.[271]

Where a statute is silent on its words or terms, another statute enacted by the Legislature, mandates that the intent of the Legislature's statute be determined by giving words their ordinary and plain meaning.[272] The dictionary is often the source referred to by the Courts to determine the ordinary meaning of a word or terms.[273]

Webster's dictionary defines "function" as "the action for which a person or thing is specially fitted or used or for which a thing exists: Purpose."[274]

This definition, or any similar dictionary definition, coupled with the inherent focus of a school to educate, would very likely result in a "school function" being classified as any event or activity, formal or informal, reasonably linked to the school, and its purpose of education, formally or informally arranged, controlled, or promoted by the school, which include events from a bake sale to a high school prom.

VII.   Federal Law on Guns in School Zones.

Under its inherent authority under the Commerce Clause, Congress has also enacted legislation precluding guns in school zones[275] based on Congressional findings that this is necessary.[276]

Thus, depending on the facts, such a crime also could be prosecuted under federal law. In most circumstances, however, local law enforcement will handle gun-in-school matters, with such crimes typically being prosecuted in the Indiana state courts.

This federal criminal law, specifically, makes it unlawful for any individual to knowingly or intentionally possess a firearm that the individual knows, or has reasonable cause to believe, is in a school zone.[277]

There are several exceptions (general and/or affirmative

defenses) to this federal criminal statutory scheme:

First, federal law does not apply to private property, which is not a part of the school grounds.

Second, the preclusion does not apply to a person with a state-issued firearm's license.

Third, it does not apply to a firearm that is not loaded, in a locked container.

Fourth, it does not apply to a firearm for use in a program approved by the school in the school zone.

Fifth, the rule does not apply to any person who is acting in accordance with a contract entered into between a school in the school zone and the individual or an employer of the individual, if the contract necessitates carry of a handgun.

Sixth, a law enforcement officer acting in his/her official capacity may possess a firearm in school zones.

Seventh, it is lawful to carry a handgun that is unloaded and is possessed while traversing school premises for the purpose of gaining access to public or private lands open to hunting, but only if the entry in the school zone is approved by the school authorities.[278]

A person convicted of carrying a firearm in a school zone shall be fined or imprisoned, for not more than five years, or both.[279]

VIII.   Carry Protocol.

Because Indiana law is generally more restrictive than federal law on this issue, this should be the first focus of the licensee. The Indiana statutory scheme provides the licensee with one narrow, but general, protocol for carrying a concealed handgun on school property or at school functions.

The protocol allows taking persons (presumably children) to and from school, or a school function, so long as the licensee is operating a motor vehicle, arrives, and drops off individuals, and then leaves, all without exiting and/or stopping the operation of the vehicle.

In all other scenarios, including on school buses, and at any school function venue at any time, the licensee must properly store his/her handgun in advance.

IX.   Conclusion.

As a matter of Indiana law, a licensee shall not possess a handgun on school property, in a school, at a school function, or on a school bus. Finally, under federal law, a person may not possess a firearm in a school zone.

A licensee must remember that he/she must comply with the requirements of both Indiana and federal law, whichever is more restrictive.

74

Chapter 6

Airports and Airplanes

> An airplane has just crashed into a tower of the World Trade Center in New York City.
> —CNN, September 11, 2001

I.   Introduction.

Following the events of September 11, 2001, perhaps no issue has ever received as much national attention as weapons at airports and on airplanes.

Therefore, it is not surprising that Indiana has a specific statutory scheme that prohibits firearms from secured areas at airports[280] and on airplanes[281], unless exempted.[282] There is substantial overlap with federal criminal laws pertaining to firearms at airports and on airplanes.

A person violating this proscription and attempting to take a firearm through a baggage check point and/or onto a flight, would likely be charged and convicted under Indiana or federal law.

There is no Indiana or federal exception recognizing an Indiana license. Thus, a licensee cannot take a handgun through a controlled area of an airport or onto an airplane.

II.   Selected Statutory Text.

"A person. . . [shall not board] a commercial or charter aircraft having in his possession a firearm."[283]

"A person . . . [shall not] knowingly or intentionally . . . [enter] an area of an airport to which access is controlled by the inspection of persons and property while the person . . . possesses . . .a firearm."[284]

III.   Crime and Punishment.

A.   Crime.

1.   Boarding Aircraft.

A person found to be carrying a handgun and boarding a commercial or charter aircraft, would be arrested, prosecuted, and convicted, all as a Class C felony.[285]

2.   Entering Controlled Area.

Carrying a firearm into and beyond a controlled area of an airport subjects the possessor to arrest, prosecution, and conviction of a Class A misdemeanor.[286]

B.   Burden of Proof.

With regard to both crimes, the prosecution has the burden to prove the elements of crime beyond a reasonable doubt.[287]

C.   Defenses.

1.   Strict Liability for Boarding.

The crime of boarding an aircraft with a firearm does not have an intent[288] element enumerated[289] and appears to impose strict liability.[290]

2.   Intent for Controlled Area.

An element of the crime of entering a controlled area of an airport with a firearm is that it be "knowing or intentional". This may give the defendant a potential defense based on forgetting the firearm was in his/her possession. Furthermore, given heightened security, the secured or controlled area of an airport may change widely and frequently.

However, it is unlikely that jurors would give this type of defense great weight, given the strong national feeling about weapons on aircraft post-September 11, 2001. Further, the prosecution would also likely make a powerful argument that it is simply inconceivable that this could be an unintentional act given that any defendant would have many "memory flags" as he/she approached the controlled area: signage, metal detectors, and Transportation Security Administration ("TSA") employees. Finally, it must be remembered that the *mens rea* element may be established by inference.[291]

D.   Punishment.

1.   Boarding.

A Class C felony carries a presumptive sentence of four years in prison, with aggravating circumstances allowing up to an additional four years or mitigating circumstances subtracting up to two years, all from the presumptive sentence.[292]

2.   Entering Controlled Area.

If convicted, this crime constitutes a Class A misdemeanor. A Class A misdemeanor carries a presumptive prison sentence of up to one year of incarceration.[293]

IV.   What Are Included Airports and Flights.

The apparent limits of this statute (and its federal counter-parts) appear to be few. The only obvious exception would be for certain private flights and private airports in certain factual scenarios, subject to other laws.

V.   Federal Law on Guns at Airports and on Airplanes.

There are comparable statutes on weapons at airports and on airplanes under federal law. This is discussed more fully in Chapter 12 on Mass Transportation.

VI.   Carry Protocol.

It is the author's belief that there is perhaps no crime that evokes any deeper feeling of ill, than a person caught with a weapon at an airport. Our society has exhibited a zero-tolerance stance.

The proper course of action is to properly stow the weapon at home. Although Indiana law does not appear to preclude storage of the weapon in one's vehicle while at any airport, nor preclude carry within common (not controlled) areas of an airport, this is simply not worth the risk. Furthermore, the federal law emerging on mass transportation also may put the licensee at criminal risk by this action.

VII.   Conclusion.

As a matter of Indiana and federal law, a licensee may not carry a handgun at and beyond any controlled area of an airport or onto an airplane.

80

Chapter 7

State Fairgrounds

> The Indiana State Fair is held for 12 days each
> summer, and has over 750,000 visitors each year.
> –Indiana State Fair Website, January, 2004

I.   Introduction.

The Legislature created a statutory State Fair Commission[294] to operate and develop the fairgrounds (and the other owned properties) for the maximum utilization of the citizens of Indiana.[295]

Within its statutory empowerment, the State Fair Commission has promulgated several administrative rules to try to meet this goal, including one prohibiting deadly weapons on the fairgrounds,[296] unless excepted from its coverage by legal status/standing (police officer).

The scope of this rule applicable to the licensee is quite narrow and only applies to the annual state fair.

II.   Selected Administrative Code Text.

"No person in possession of a deadly weapon shall be permitted onto or be permitted to remain on the fairgrounds during the annual state fair."[297]

III.   Remedy for Violation.

The State Fair Commission's rule is civil in nature (insofar as practically applied to a licensee) to allow it to control and develop the fairgrounds.

Thus, any licensee in violation of this rule would be subject to confiscation of his/her deadly weapon and ejection from the fairgrounds by fair personnel, security, or the many working police in attendance at the fair.

Any unlicenced person caught in violation of this rule, would be subject, additionally, to arrest for carrying a handgun without a license as a matter of criminal law.

IV. What Constitutes Annual Indiana Fair.

This administrative rule is quite limited in scope, and only applies to the annual state fair.[298] Thus, the numerous other events that are venued at the fairgrounds throughout the year, would not be subject to this rule. Presumably, the annual state fair restriction to carry would encompass the period from the advertised opening date and time, to its closing date and time.

V. Carry Protocol.

This administrative rule specifically includes what a licensee should do if faced with being at the annual state fair and in possession of his/her handgun.

Specifically, the rule indicates that the licensee should stow the handgun in his/her vehicle and out of view. Thus, the rule appears to technically allow the licensee to arrive at the fairgrounds of the annual state fair, as long as the handgun remains in the vehicle.

In practice, and lawful application, the weapon should not only be locked in the vehicle and out of sight, but fully secured in an auto safe.

The licensee should also consider leaving his/her weapon properly secured at home.

VI.   Conclusion.

Given the thousands upon thousands of people who flock to the annual state fair, it is not surprising that the State Fair Commission has enacted this rule for the security of such a large crowd.

The licensee should be cognizant of this rule in order to comply with the law, but should also recognize its narrow scope. All of the other annual events held at the state fairgrounds are not subject to this exclusion, nor could they be as a practical matter. In fact, there are several gun and knife shows at the state fairgrounds over the course of any given year.

84

Chapter   8

Riverboat Casinos

> For Fiscal Year 2003, Indiana's 10 Riverboat Casinos had combined total admissions of over 26 million people, with total state-wide wins of over 2.1 billion dollars.
> –Indiana Gaming Commission, Annual Report to the Governor, Fiscal Year 2003, Pgs. 24, 26

I.   Introduction.

Anyone who has ever watched a television documentary, or explored the history of the gaming industry, understands that it has a long and bloody history connected with corruption, firearms, and violence.

Therefore, it is not surprising that when the Legislature legalized riverboat gaming, and created the Indiana Gaming Commission, that it would address firearms,[299] as gaming is now a highly regulated industry.[300]

There is no exception for the licensee to carry on the riverboat itself, and the exception for law enforcement officers is quite narrow.

II.   Selected Administrative Code Text.

"No individual . . . shall carry a weapon on board the riverboat during any excursion."[301]

III.   Remedy for Violation.

The Indiana Gaming Commission's rule is civil in nature to effectuate tight control over the gaming area.

To make this point, the Indiana Gaming Commission requires the riverboat licensee (holding a casino license, not to be confused with a handgun license) to post a sign at the point of passenger entry into the casino containing the following language:

"No weapons are allowed beyond this point. Failure to comply with this rule may result in the immediate removal from the riverboat, immediate detention by security personnel, the imposition of civil penalties or exclusion under IC 4-33."[302]

Thus, any licensee found in violation of this rule would be subject to confiscation of their deadly weapon and ejection from the riverboat and casino property, by security personnel or police.

Any person violating this rule, and not a permit holder, would be subject, additionally, to arrest for carrying a handgun without a license as a matter of criminal law. [303]

IV.   What Constitutes Carry Limits at Riverboat.

The Indiana Gaming Commission rule is limited in scope, and would not preclude the patron-licensee from having a handgun anywhere in the casino complex (hotel), except the actual point of boarding the riverboat and beyond, subject to any other law, rules, and regulations.

V.   Carry Protocol.

Aside from the obvious choices that the licensee may properly stow his firearm at home or in his/her vehicle, the Indiana Gaming Commission, in perhaps a recognition of the number of individuals that have handgun licenses in Indiana, requires the riverboat owner to have a weapons check:

"The riverboat licensee shall provide a secure place to which patrons do not have access, to store weapons checked by patrons, off duty law enforcement officers, or off duty federal enforcement officers."[304]

VI.   Conclusion.

A licensee may carry his/her handgun to an Indiana riverboat casino, subject to any other law, but the Indiana Gaming Commission precludes the possessor from carrying the weapon at and beyond the point of boarding the riverboat.

Chapter 9

Maritime Ports

"In 1999, the firms and operations at the three public ports managed by the Indiana Port Commission contributed approximately $1.452 billion of economic activity to the development of the state. The activities of the ports also contributed:
- over $398 million in wages for Indiana workers
- an estimated 10,503 direct and indirect jobs
- over $22 million in tax revenue for the state of Indiana
- nearly $1.4 million in local property taxes
- an additional $54 million of economic impact attributable to publicly funded construction projects completed in 1999."

–Indiana Port Commission Economic Impact (2004)

I. Introduction.

In 1961, to promote agricultural, industrial, and commercial development of Indiana's waterways, the Legislature created the Indiana Port Commission.[305] The charge of the Indiana Port Commission is to work with the federal government to construct and operate commercial ports on Lake Michigan, the Ohio River, or the Wabash River.[306]

The Indiana Port Commission has enacted several administrative rules[307] to regulate its ports,[308] including rules precluding firearms at port facilities, unless a person is excepted by their legal standing/status (police officer).[309] There are no

89

exceptions for Indiana licensees for carry on these ports.

II.   Selected Administrative Code Text.

"No person . . .shall carry any firearms, concealed weapons, explosives, or similar inflammable materials on the port area."[310]

"No person shall transport or carry on the port property any of the following . . .(2) firearms . . . ."[311]

III.   Remedy for Violation.

These administrative rules are also silent as to their remedy for violation, but being civil in nature as applied to a licensee, would clearly include expulsion from the port area, and, likely, confiscation of the firearm. Furthermore, to the extent that the port property comes within federal jurisdiction, federal criminal or civil penalties may also apply.[312]

Any person found in violation of the Indiana Port Commission's administrative rule, and not a licensee, would additionally be subject to arrest for carrying a handgun without a license,[313] as a matter of Indiana criminal law.

IV.   What Constitutes a Port.

The statutory definition of the term "port,"[314] for purposes of the Indiana Port Commission's charge, is substantially broader than the three ports actually under the Indiana Port Commission's jurisdiction,[315] which are as follows:

1.   Indiana's International Port/Burns Harbor at Portage
        6625 South Boundary Drive
        Portage, Indiana 46368
        (219) 787-8636

2.   Clark Maritime Center
        5100 Port Road
        Jeffersonville, Indiana 47130
        (812) 283-9662

3.   Southwind Maritime Center
        2751 Bluff Road
        Mount Vernon, Indiana 47620
        (812) 838-4382

[!] CAUTION, Expanding Powers of Indiana Port Commission: Under statutory changes in 2003, the Indiana Port Commission's powers were expanded, and thus the licensee must always be cognizant of any other areas that may be subject to the Indiana Port Commission's administrative rules. How this will develop, and other areas of restriction, are not presently defined.[316]

V.   Carry Protocol.

The licensee has three clear choices in order to comply with the Indiana Port Commission's rules. The first would be to properly secure the handgun at the licensee's home.

A second, but unclear matter, would be if the licensee could park on non-port property and properly secure the weapon in his/her vehicle. Again, as with all instances of carrying a handgun, planning is the key to adhering to the law.

Third, the Indiana Port Commission has considered the scenario of a licensee coming to a port with a firearm. Thus, a "weapons check" is a part of the administrative rule on ports:

"(b) All persons other than the excepted classes [which does not include licensees] shall: (1) surrender all objects described in subsection (a) [including handguns] to the port security guard at the entrance gate or to the port director; (2) be given a receipt; and (3) recover the object upon leaving the port area and surrendering the receipt."[317]

VI. Conclusion.

An Indiana handgun license is not valid for carry in and at maritime ports of the Indiana Port Commission located at Portage, Indiana; Jeffersonville, Indiana; and Mount Vernon, Indiana.

Chapter 10

State Courthouses and/or Courtrooms

> "It is obviously appropriate to forbid litigants, witnesses, and spectators to bring firearms into the courtroom. It is equally obvious that because of the potential for harm, coming into a courtroom armed is a matter of grave concern."
> –*Macon v. Indiana*, 629 N.E.2d 883, 885 (Ind.Ct.App. 1994)

I.   Introduction.

The rule of law is what, arguably, separates any organized society from chaos and anarchy. As such, the judicial system, through its courts, usually becomes the final arbitrator of disputes. Furthermore, many, if not most, legal matters involve very emotional and high-stake issues. Based on this, firearms have no place in Indiana courthouses and/or courtrooms.

While there are states that have a statutory criminal preclusion[318] against firearms in courthouses and/or courtrooms, this is not the case in Indiana. As such, the authority to limit a licensee from carrying a handgun into a courthouse and/or courtroom is not as clearly defined.

However, there are several sources of authority for these restrictions, and it is clear that a licensee may not carry a handgun, or other weapon, around, at, or in any Indiana courthouse and/or courtroom. Moreover, in most circumstances, the typical exception for law enforcement officers does not apply if he/she is a litigant or party to a case.

II.   Selected Statutory Text and Court Rules.

The authority for trial courts to preclude firearms, and all other weapons from Indiana courthouses and/or courtrooms, and to enforce this prohibition, emanates from three sources: (1) statute; (2) rules of trial practice; and (3) the inherent authority of courts.

A.   Statutory Text.

"Other Indiana courts may establish rules for their own government, supplementary to and not conflicting with the rules prescribed by the supreme court or any statute."[319]

B.   Trial Rules and Local Rules.

"Each local court may from time to time make and amend rules governing its practice not inconsistent with these rules."[320]

C.   Inherent Court Powers and Standing Orders.

Finally, the largely unwritten rules of judicial practice and protocol, along with the inherent authority of trial courts to run their affairs in an orderly and safe fashion, in furtherance of this statutory and trial rule authority, allow standing orders, or other orders, to be adopted by individual courts.

These orders and standing orders may not necessarily be reduced to local rules and forwarded to the Supreme Court. Further, local rules, standing orders, or other orders are not published in any singular reference format.[321]

In particular, standing orders may simply be posted on courthouse building doors or outside of a particular courtroom. (*See* Appendix "6" for Marion County's standing Order on Firearms and Weapons). Typically, such orders and/or standing orders are the means by which Indiana trial courts have addressed firearms in, at, and around Indiana courthouses.

III.   Remedy for Violation.

It must be presumed that a local rule, standing order, or other prohibition exists against carry. Furthermore, each licensee may be deemed to be on constructive notice of this fact.[322]

The enforcement of trial courts' local rules and orders is through its contempt powers. Typically, direct contempt is how Indiana trial court judges have responded to handguns being brought into courthouses and/or courtrooms. [323]

Direct contempt involves action(s) occurring near the court that interferes with the business of the court, and of which the judge has personal knowledge. Direct contempt subjects the person to fine or imprisonment. Destruction of the handgun would also be likely.

These contempt issues would presumably have an intent element, requiring the willful nature of the contempt and determination of the court. However, indirect contempt would still exist for violation of a standing order outside of the presence of the court.

The cases decided by the Courts have taken issue with direct contempt for mere possession of a firearm in a courtroom.

However, these cases are older, and given the current security focus of all branches of government, the author believes the courts will effectively lower the threshold intent element of contempt in such situations.

IV.   What Constitutes a Courthouse and/or Courtroom.

It is important to note that as courts have become separated from the traditional county seat and courthouse, many courts have come to exist in non-traditional facilities. Thus, the licensee must always contemplate the location of courthouses and/or courtrooms and their corresponding property.

V.   Carry Protocol.

The licensee going to a courthouse and/or courtroom must plan ahead. The best solution is for the handgun to be left at its normal place of storage, which is presumably one's home in a safe. In the event that this is not possible, then the licensee should stow the handgun in his/her vehicle and park only in public, non-government parking. Parking on courthouse grounds may cause a violation of the applicable rule.

> [†] **PRACTICAL TIP, Additional Court Security:** As noted in the introduction, courthouses and/or courtrooms are often emotionally charged environments with unique safety issues. When a licensee is faced with specific security concerns, the matter is easily resolved by telephoning the particular court, which allows the court to make advance arrangements for additional security in the courtroom. The author has utilized this technique many times, and the courts

have always been receptive to being proactive in response to any security issues.

VI.   Conclusion.

As a practical matter, most courthouses now have metal detectors that require screening before entrance, precluding carrying into a courthouse. Thus, indirect contempt may be a more likely possibility. In any event, the handgun would be confiscated and destroyed. In short, handguns, and any and all other weapons, are not allowed around, at or in Indiana courthouses and/or courtrooms.

Chapter 11

Federal Property

> "This constitution, and the laws of the United
> States which shall be made in pursuance thereof;
> and all treaties made, or which shall be made,
> under the authority of the United States, shall be
> the supreme law of the land; and the judges in
> every state shall be bound thereby, anything in the
> constitution or laws of any state to the contrary
> notwithstanding."
> –United States Constitution, Supremacy Clause,
> Article VI, Clause 2

I.   Introduction.

The federal government has the right to regulate affairs on its property. Using its legislative powers, the Congress has enacted civil and/or criminal statutes precluding firearms on federal property.[324]

There is a very limited exception to allow a firearm on federal property for lawful hunting.[325]   The statutory exceptions to the prohibition against carrying a handgun at federal facilities (and courts), which can include law enforcement officers, provides no other exceptions for the licensee.[326]

More specifically, an Indiana license is not recognized on federal property.

II.   Selected Statutory Text.

". . .[W]hoever knowingly possesses or causes to be present a firearm in a Federal facility (other than a Federal court facility) or attempts to do so, shall be fined under this title or imprisoned . . ."[327]

III.   Crime and Punishment.

A.   Crime, Fine, and Sentence.

A person (licensee or not) carrying, or attempting to carry, a handgun into a federal facility would be subject to arrest, confiscation of the weapon, prosecution, and face a fine and/or incarceration for up to one year.[328]

B.   Statutory Enhancements.

This crime is subject to two significant enhancements.[329] The first is intending to use the firearm in the commission of a crime in a federal facility, which by itself (not considering the crime committed), subjects the offender to fine and/or imprisonment for up to five years.[330] The second is applicable to intentionally taking a weapon into a federal court facility.[331] This subjects the defendant to imprisonment for up to two years and a fine.[332]

C.   Burden of Proof.

The prosecution, as with all state-level crimes, would have the burden of proof beyond a reasonable doubt.[333]

D.   Defenses.

There are three apparent defenses to violation of this federal law precluding firearms at federal facilities and federal courts.

1.   Lack of Intent.

The first is a general criminal defense, as the crime requires that the prosecution prove the act was "knowingly". This is the *mens rea* component of this crime.[334]

2.   Lack of Notice.

Secondly, the statutory scheme precludes conviction and fine, unless there is notice "conspicuously" posted at each public entrance to a federal facility or federal court. This is an affirmative defense to the crime. However, if there is no notice posted, but the possessor of the firearm had actual notice that the facility was a federal facility or a federal court, and that firearms were not permitted, the crime lies.[335] This is an affirmative defense.

3.   Lawful Hunting.

The third is an affirmative defense if the handgun is possessed on federal property incident to lawful hunting.[336]

IV.   What Constitutes Federal Property.

The scope and outside limitations of this preclusion of handguns on federal property are apparently quite broad and undefined. A "federal facility" is defined as property where federal employees are regularly present to perform official duties. This includes owned and leased property.

Because the licensee has no effective way of knowing if federal employees regularly perform duties at any given federal facility, the only "safe" course of action is to not carry a weapon onto any federal property, except incident to lawful hunting.

The law is further problematic for a licensee, because of the mixed use buildings where there may be federal offices located in privately owned/leased buildings. At a minimum in this situation, the licensee would be precluded from taking the firearm into the official offices. Common areas of such buildings are an open issue.

As with Indiana law, Congress can delegate authority to administrative agencies, which may enact rules and regulations regarding firearms. Federal administrative bodies have done so in many circumstances. These rules and regulations addressing firearms, are important, but are beyond the scope of this Book.

This is because it is clear that the licensee may not possess firearms or other weapons on federal property. However, one such common administrative rule, further regulating firearms on federal property, is again noted in the text for instructional purposes. This is the Postal Service administrative rule that precludes firearms on postal property.[337]

Also, given the separation of powers between the three branches of government, and in recognition of the inherent powers of federal courts, the Congress specifically enumerates in its statute that federal courts retain the ability to additionally regulate firearms in the courts by contempt powers, orders, and regulations.

Federal properties and included offices that may be commonly encountered by the licensee are as follows:

- Federal courts and court buildings
- Military bases
- Federal buildings (housing federal agencies)
- Social Security offices
- IRS offices
- FBI offices
- Secret Service offices
- U.S. Attorney offices
- DEA offices
- ATF offices[338]

V.   Carry Protocol.

There is no provision allowing any Indiana citizen, licensee or not, to take a handgun onto any federal property, save incident to lawful hunting. Furthermore, there is no provision to allow such a handgun to be left in his/her vehicle if parked on federal property.

Thus, the licensee must plan in advance and either leave his/her handgun properly stowed at home, or park on non-federal property and properly stow his/her weapon in the vehicle before entering.

VI.   Conclusion.

Carrying a concealed handgun onto federal property and/or into a federal court, where federal employees are regularly employed, whether or not a person is an Indiana licensee is a criminal act and must be avoided. There is one narrow exception for lawful hunting.

Chapter 12

Mass Transportation

> "The term 'mass transportation' means transportation by a conveyance that provides regular and continuing general or special transportation to the public, but does not include a school bus, charter, or sightseeing transportation."
> –49 U.S.C. § 5302(a)(7)
>
> ". . .[T]he term 'mass transportation' has the meaning given to that term in section 5302(a)(7) of title 49, United States Code, except that the term shall include school bus, charter, and sightseeing transportation . . . ."
> –18 U.S.C. § 1993(c)(5)

I.   Introduction.

The point of departure in understanding the limits (present and future) on carrying weapons to mass transportation facilities and/ or on mass transportation vehicles is with a discussion of the DHS.

Following the September 11, 2001, terrorist attacks, the DHS was established. The DHS was created to encompass all twenty-two federal agencies with a role in protecting the nation's transportation system, territorial waters, and borders, under one umbrella.[339]

II.   Creation of TSA.

Upon creation of the DHS, its charge was to utilize the benefits of inter-agency resources, cooperation, and accountability under its umbrella to prevent or reduce future domestic terrorist attacks, and minimize the impact of such attacks.

Under the complex organizational structure of the DHS, the Border and Transportation Security Directorate encompasses the mass transportation element of security through the TSA, which is an administration of the Department of Transportation.

Effectively, the TSA acts as an enabler for mass transportation security. However, actual breaches of federal statutory law and/or its rules and/or regulations are typically addressed through local, state, and federal law enforcement officers, and state prosecutors and/or the Department of Justice.

This is a rapidly evolving area of law as the TSA implements rules and regulations to secure mass transportation. However, it is anticipated that the TSA and/or Congress will ultimately, criminally prohibit all firearms from being carried on mass transportation in passenger areas. This, of course, would exclude those individuals normally excepted from such preclusions (police officers and federal agents).

Due to the scope of the TSA's authority, and its anticipated future acts to protect mass transportation, a chapter is dedicated to this topic in this annual Book. Thus, as the law evolves, so will this chapter.

The present limitations regarding firearms on mass transportation are of three substantial types: (1) mass carrier rules and regulations; (2) federal law (and Indiana law as noted in Chapter 6) on firearms at airports and on airplanes; and (3) preclusion of a "destructive device" around, at, or in mass transportation carrier terminals and/or vehicles.

Even if a mass transportation facility and/or vehicle is in Indiana or a reciprocal state, federal law does not recognize an Indiana-issued handgun license in these restricted areas. Thus, while a given state's laws may not be violated by having a valid license and a lawfully possessed handgun, a federal crime may stand.

III. Mass Carrier Rules and Regulations.

The TSA clearly notes on its website that effectively all carriers have rules and regulations that would deny boarding to a guest with a handgun, and/or subject any possessor to expulsion from the mass transportation facility and/or vehicle.

This includes, but is not limited to, trains, planes, buses, cruise ships, and the like. Such rules and regulations may be accessed by and through the TSA's website, which has related links to most major mass carriers and/or their trade organizations.[340]

IV. Airports and Aircraft.

With regard to commercial flight, a person attempting to bring a firearm onto the flight would be subject to arrest, confiscation of the weapon, and prosecution. The defendant could be charged under Indiana or federal law (*See* Chapter 6 for Indiana law on same).

Any person on, or attempting to board an aircraft intended for operation in air transportation that has on or about the individual, or in the property of the individual, a concealed or dangerous weapon that would be accessible to the person in flight, is subject to a fine and/or imprisonment for not more than ten years, or both.[341]

V.   Terrorism Against Mass Transportation.

An unsettled area of law, insofar as carrying a handgun is concerned, is how the federal terrorist act against mass transportation will be ultimately applied. This statute makes it a crime to willfully place a destructive device in, upon, or near a mass transportation vehicle or ferry.[342]

While it appears that Congressional history would have precluded a "handgun" from being included within this definition, the definition of "destructive device" is somewhat unclear as to this issue.[343] Specifically, any .50 caliber handgun, or handgun with a ½ inch or bigger bore, would technically be included within the term "destructive device".

Under this statutory prohibition, to the extent it is applied to handguns, a person carrying a handgun may not be able to be around a mass transportation facility, such as a public parking area at the location. A conviction under this statute is subject to a fine and/or imprisonment of not more than twenty years.[344]

VI.   Carry Protocol.

It is not anticipated that federal law will ultimately preclude a lawfully possessed handgun from being properly stowed in a vehicle in a common parking lot of a mass transportation facility. Further, it is not anticipated that a possessor could not drop off a person at such a facility while possessing a handgun in a public drop off and pick up point, particularly if remaining in his/her vehicle.

However, at present, the risks are simply too high to take until the matter is further clarified, given the lengthy jail sentence possible and our society's zero-tolerance policy toward transportation security. The licensee is advised in all circumstances to properly stow the handgun at home.

VII.   Conclusion.

With regard to all forms of mass transportation, it appears that no firearm may be taken aboard, either as a matter of Indiana or federal law. Furthermore, most all carriers have policies against such carry. Clearly, the matter is an Indiana and federal criminal act, insofar as controlled areas of airports and airplanes are concerned.

Finally, depending upon how the terrorism statute is applied to mass transportation, it may be a federal criminal act to have handguns of certain calibers around, at, or in a mass transportation terminal or vehicle.

An Indiana licensee has no right to carry his/her handgun upon any mass transportation facility or in any mass transportation vehicle. The firearm should be secured and stored before going to any mass transportation point.

110

Chapter 13

Private Property

> "The relation of landlord and tenant normally arises from a contract whereby the owner of an estate in land transfers a possessory interest . . .in the whole of the land, or in a designated space in the land, or in a building on the land, to a transferee in return for a consideration which is usually the payment of, or agreement to pay, rent."
> –Cornelius J. Moynihan, *Introduction to the Law of Real Property* 56 (2d ed. West, 1988)

I.   Introduction.

Private property is not typically considered in the analysis of the restrictions on the carrying of a handgun, although it should be. A licensee may not be able to lawfully carry a handgun onto private property, or may face restrictions on carry, for a variety of reasons.

Specifically, the legal nature of an owner or possessor's interest in the real property, coupled with his/her position regarding allowing firearms on the property, dictates the limitations, if any, on the carrying of a handgun by those entering upon the land.

The licensee would likely encounter limits on the carry of a handgun on private property in two contexts: (1) work; and (2) the ability to enter, or remain on, other private property while carrying a handgun.

[!] **CAUTION, Private Property Limits Must Be Considered with Other Restrictions:** It must be remembered that carry of a handgun on private property may be subject to all of the foregoing Indiana and federal, civil and criminal, limitations.

II.   Selected Caselaw on Private Property.

The Indiana Court of Appeals perhaps best summarized an owner's vast rights regarding regulation of persons on their property:

"Neither Indiana, federal, or common law grants Indiana citizens a property interest in access to private property. At common law, a proprietor of a privately-owned amusement may exclude whomever he wishes for any reason, or for no reason whatsoever."[345]

III.   What Constitutes a Real Property Interest.

The following analysis only applies if a licensee has an ownership or possessory interest in the property in question.

A person with a real property interest is typically by actual ownership or lease. Such interests may be fragmented in several ways among individuals. Any such owner or lessee may impose rules and prohibitions regarding the carry of a handgun on their property.

The limits on carry of a handgun on private real property may become a complex question of contract and property law, especially where a lease of the property is involved. However, the example of a typical lease of real property is provided to give the licensee a model of how to properly analyze property interests and carry of a handgun.

A.   Lessor/Lessee.

Conceptually, leaseholds may be best understood in relation to the right to restrict the carry of a handgun thereon, by considering the nature of the property holder's interest, lessor to lessee.

A leasehold interest (such as lease of an apartment or business office/building) is a conveyance of an interest in real property for a limited time. However, the conveyance between lessor (owner of the property) and lessee (renter of the property) is a matter of contract law (the lease).

As such, either the lessor or lessee can address the use and/or the restricted use of the property in the lease. One such restriction may be firearms.

1.   Lease Restrictions.

Specifically, a lease may preclude or allow firearms on the premise/land as a matter of contract law. Among other things, failure to adhere to the terms of a lease addressing firearms, could allow the other party to the lease to sue for breach of the lease, or seek an injunction.

Aside from the private property interest held by the lessor and lessee, any other person on the property would not be excluded from criminal law, and would have to adhere to the requirement of licensing or be subject to arrest.

Finally, the lessee, subject to any limitations contained in the lease, would have the ability to place any restrictions on those coming onto the property insofar as carrying a handgun is concerned.

For instance, a gun range lessee could require those entering the range to only have unloaded guns, except on the firing line.

> **[?] EXAMPLE, Commercial Real Estate Lease for Gun Store:** As an example from the author's practice, a lease was presented for review by a relocating gun shop owner. On review, the proposed lease included contractual paragraphs prohibiting the lessee from having firearms on the premises. This may be and/or become a standard provision due to insurance restrictions faced by lessors. Ultimately, these preclusions were deleted, and replaced with provisions specifically allowing firearms on the leased premises by lessee. Had the lease been executed without these changes, it would have precluded firearms from the premises.

IV.   Classification of Person Entering Land.

The following analysis only applies if a licensee has no legal ownership or possessory interest in the property he/she is entering.

An owner or lessee's ability to restrict (or be restricted) concerning the carry of a handgun on his/her property may be further expanded or limited by the status of the person entering onto the land.

In Indiana, a person entering upon the land of another comes onto the land as an invitee, a licensee, or a trespasser.[346] This classification may, in part, determine the right to carry a handgun.

A.   Licensee.

A license to do some act on the land of another is not an interest in real property. It legally gives the licensee a personal right and privilege to do an act on another's property.[347] Assuming the license did not specifically include or exclude the licensee's right to possess firearms on the property, the property possessor could limit this right in ways he/she sees proper.

> **[?] EXAMPLE, Hunting on Land of Another:** Bob has a long-term lease on 100 acres of woods. His lease does not place any restrictions on his use of the land as far as firearms or hunting are concerned. Bob then sells a license to his friend, Ted, for $100 to hunt on the land during deer season. Unless expressly limited (for bow hunting only), this license would imply the right to possess firearms by Ted on Bob's leasehold, even if it did not identify such right. A different scenario, such as a license to fish on the property, may exclude the right to possess firearms on the property by Ted.

B.   Invitee.

A person is legally classified as an invitee on the land of another if: (1) he/she enters by invitation of the possessor; (2) entry onto the land of the possessor is connected with the owner's business or with an activity the possessor conducts or allows conducted on the land; and (3) there is a benefit for both the possessor and invitee.[348]

An interest holder of the property can place any type of limits on the invitee, except those specifically limited by other law. These limits may specifically include handguns.

[?] EXAMPLE, Retail Establishments With "No Handguns Allowed" Posted at Entry: As a possessor with a real property interest, a retailer has the right to limit, and qualify the right to enter the property, subject to not carrying a handgun. It would be improper to enter, and the licensee would be subject to ejection for possession of a handgun thereat. Failure to leave once requested, would subject the licensee to arrest for criminal trespass.

1.   Employee.

An employee is classified as an invitee.[349] However, this area is specifically broken out, and discussed separately, because of great interest in this subject expressed to the author.

Unlike other invitees, an invitee-employee has more at risk than just ejection from the premises of the employer. This is especially the case because Indiana is a strong "at will" employment state.[350]

Any employee that is not under contract, may be subject to summary dismissal for possession of a handgun at the workplace, if the employer has a rule or policy against such possession.

Again, the foregoing is subject to any other law, meaning that if the terminated employee does not have a handgun permit, he/she would be subject to criminal arrest and prosecution.

C.   Trespasser.

A trespasser, in addition to being subject to civil liability for trespass on the land[351] and arrest for the crime of criminal trespass,[352] would also be subject to arrest for carrying a handgun without a license if he/she was not a licensee, if found by law enforcement officers.

V.   Governmental Unit Regulation of its Property.

While the Indiana Legislature has preempted the ability of local governments to regulate firearms, there is a narrow exception that allows municipalities to regulate firearms on their own property. There is no practical way to determine this other than by contacting the building authority for the place of carry. (*See* Questions and Answers for more discussion of this topic; *See* Appendix "7" for the Indianapolis-Marion County Building Authority Rules and Regulations Governing the City-County Building and Grounds, which covers firearms).

VI.   Carry Protocol.

If the licensee is the owner or lessee of the property, he/she may carry thereon, subject to any other law, unless limited by contract.

If the licensee is not an owner or lessee of the property, his/her rights may be limited in innumerable ways by the property owner or lessee. This may range from leaving the weapon in the licensee's vehicle upon entry on the land or not being allowed to enter with a handgun, to no restrictions at all.   The licensee's right to carry may in other ways be impacted by his/her legal classification upon entry of the land (licensee, invitee, trespasser).

Again, advanced consideration of daily events of carry must be considered, and areas of potential limitation considered.

VII.   Conclusion.

On private property, an interest holder's rights may be addressed by contract, such as between lessor and lessee. Furthermore, the status of a person entering onto the land of another, coupled with the owner or lessee's position on firearms on his/her property, determines whether a licensee can carry his/her handgun on the property, and under what circumstances. It must be remembered that all other sources of state and federal law also apply to this analysis.

PART III:
USE OF FORCE

"If a man destroy the eye of another man, they
destroy his eye."
–Hammurabi's Code (circa 2030 B.C.)

Without question, the most fundamental responsibility associated with gun ownership is the "what if" of the use of force. The time to contemplate and answer this question is long before any such event arises, lest the defender become the victim by his own weapon. Worse yet, the defender could make an error of judgment resulting in unjustified injury or loss of life, and subjecting himself/ herself to criminal and/or civil liability.

Specifically, the stressors and impaired decision-making associated with the use of force may well preclude accurate judgment without advanced thought and preparation. This is the central reason that from the lowest ranking security officer, to the most elite member of the special operations community, teaching, testing, practice, and study of such matters are of critical importance. Simply put, they are central to a successful and legally proper outcome where force is involved. The licensee prepares by understanding and contemplating the law of force.

Part III, Chapter 14, focuses on the use of force, including deadly force. Chapter 15 addresses the immediate response to the use of deadly force. This chapter will conclude with a summary of the ways criminal and/or civil component(s) of a deadly force encounter may proceed.

It is at this juncture, before turning to the specific law applicable to the use of force, that the author wants to make very clear his position regarding the use of force, including deadly force. This is, with careful planning, a civilian should almost never face a situation where the use of any force is even contemplated. Furthermore, a 911 call and law enforcement officers may be able to further reduce any perceived and/or actual risks/threats.

Specifically, even if legally justified, most all civilian uses of force could have been avoided. A human life cannot be replaced. A licensee with a cavalier or reckless attitude should not be carrying a handgun.

Finally, the use of deadly force by a civilian, justified or not, will dramatically, and in unforseen ways, negatively impact the life of the licensee. These impacts range from mental health issues to criminal and/or civil prosecution.

Chapter 14

Use of Force

> "Permitting one to threaten to use deadly force leads in dangerous progression to an unacceptable conclusion. Here, the victim would have been entitled to use deadly force to repel the perceived threat."
> –*Nantz v. State*, 740 N.E.2d 1276, 1281 (Ind.Ct.App. 2001)

I. Introduction.

In order to understand the lawful and prudent use of force, one should think of the matter as existing on a continuum,[353] with innumerable legal and factual points along the way. At one end of this continuum is the lawful and legally justified[354] use of force, while at the other, the unlawful use of force.

Within this legal continuum are factual scenarios that, while they may allow the lawful use of force, do not allow that force to be deadly in nature. This continuum is made even more complex by the fact that legal justification for the use of force can extend to third parties and/or property.

It is the scenarios between the ends of this complicated continuum that are the subject of litigation, due to a host of questions without answers: Was the use of force necessary? Was the force reasonable? Is the legal justification for the use of force inapplicable?

Stated differently, if the use of force is factually and/or legally questionable, then a prosecutor may elect to move forward with the matter.   If this is the case, the handgun user becomes the defendant, and may be charged with crimes ranging from battery to murder.

In this circumstance, the defendant would then have to raise self-defense as an affirmative criminal defense. Ultimately, a judge or jury would make a decision based on the facts of the case applied to specific legal standards.

In contrast, a prosecutor may exercise his/her discretion and not charge a crime at all in clearer cases.[355]

It is important to note that the discussion in Chapter 14 has little bearing on whether a person using force will be sued civilly for the use of that force.

II.   Selected Statutory Text.

"A person is justified in engaging in conduct otherwise prohibited if he has legal authority to do so."[356]

III.   Self-Defense.

The legal justification to do what would otherwise be a criminal act, allows a person to use force against another to protect himself/herself, third persons, and property from what is reasonably believed to be the imminent use of unlawful force.[357] This means that by statute, the person applying force has an affirmative criminal defense to the crimes that could be charged in connection with the application of the force.

A.   Elements.

The affirmative criminal defense of self-defense is successfully established if the defendant: (1) acted without fault, (2) was in a place where he had a right to be, and (3) was in reasonable fear of death or great bodily harm.[358]

1.   Reasonableness of Fear.

One of the most challenged elements of self-defense is if the defendant was in "reasonable fear". When a person uses force, the court and/or jury will look at the situation as it would reasonably appear to the person being attacked, all to determine what force was necessary to resist the attack.   Factually, the reasonableness of the fear is determined from the standpoint, and through the eyes, of the person being attacked, under consideration of all existing circumstances.[359]

> **[!] CAUTION, Reasonable Fear in Criminal Practice:** In actual criminal trial practice, what defendants believe is "reasonable fear" often substantially differs from what a jury views as "reasonable fear". Hundreds of inmates in Indiana jails believed their use of force was "reasonable". A jury, however, did not. In no uncertain terms, force situations must be avoided. Even "textbook" use of force may not be considered reasonable by a jury.

B.   Burden of Proof.

1.   Prosecution's Burden.

Once a defendant asserts a claim of self-defense, the

prosecution must disprove, beyond a reasonable doubt, at least one of the elements of the affirmative defense of self-defense.[360]

2. Affirmative Defense Rebuttal.

The state may meet its burden by either rebutting the affirmative defense directly or relying on the sufficiency of the evidence in its case-in-chief.[361]

IV. Use of Force to Protect Person.

The legal justification to use force, including deadly force in certain contexts, is applicable to the use of force to protect oneself, a third party, or to prevent a forcible felony.[362]

Specifically, a person is justified in using reasonable force against another person if the person reasonably believes the imminent use of unlawful force.[363]

A. Third Persons.

The right to use force to defend oneself also applies to the right to defend third parties.[364]

B. Deadly Force.

A person may use deadly force only if he/she reasonably believes that such force is necessary to prevent death or serious bodily injury to himself/herself, a third party, or to stop a forcible felony.[365]

1.   Serious Bodily Injury.

Serious bodily injury means an injury that creates a substantial risk of death or that causes: (1) serious permanent disfigurement, (2) unconsciousness, (3) extreme pain, (4) permanent or protracted loss or impairment of the function of bodily member or organ, or (5) loss of a fetus.[366]

2.   Forcible Felony.

A forcible felony is a felonious act that involves the use or threat of force against a human being, or in which there is imminent danger of bodily injury to a human being.[367]

V.   Use of Force to Protect Dwelling.

With regard to one's home, a person is justified in using reasonable force, including deadly force, if the person reasonably believes that the force is necessary to prevent or terminate the other person's unlawful entry of, or attack on, his/her dwelling or curtilage.[368]

A.   Definition of Dwelling.

A dwelling is a building, structure, or other enclosed space, permanent or temporary, movable or fixed, that is a person's home or place of lodging.[369]

B.   Definition of Curtilage.

The term "curtilage" has been defined as follows:

"Curtilage [is defined] . . . as the space of ground adjoining the dwelling house used in connection therewith in the conduct of family affairs and for carrying on domestic purposes, usually including the buildings occupied in connection with the dwelling house. It is the propinquity to a dwelling and the use in connection with it for family purposes which is to be regarded."[370]

> **[!] CAUTION, Application of Curtilage Strictly Construed:** The doctrine of protecting one's outer property connected with the dwelling house (not apartment) is centuries old and derived in and thrived under a time much different from today, all when the general society was more rural and agrarian.[371] It is the author's opinion, that the Courts will narrowly and strictly apply this legal justification. Thus, this affirmative defense in protection of curtilage may not be successful in a criminal prosecution.

VI.   Use of Force to Protect Non-Dwelling Property.

There is also statutory authority to use reasonable force to protect property other than a dwelling or curtilage. Specifically, if a person reasonably believes that the force is necessary to immediately prevent, or terminate the other person's trespass on, or criminal interference with, property lawfully in the person's possession, a member of the person's immediate family, or belonging to a person whose property the person has authority to protect, reasonable force may be used.[372]

A.   Deadly Force Not Permitted.

Unless it involves protecting the person, a third party,

or a dwelling/curtilage, as discussed above, deadly force is not permitted.[373]

VII.   Use of Force to Prevent Hijacking of Aircraft.

In clear response to the events of September 11, 2001, the Legislature amended the statute authorizing force to encompass air piracy. Thus, a person is justified in using reasonable force, including deadly force, against another person, if the person reasonably believes that such force is necessary to prevent or stop another from hijacking, attempting to hijack, or otherwise seizing, or attempting to seize, unlawful control of an aircraft in flight.[374]

VIII.   Use of Force Relating to Arrest or Escape.

A person who is not a law enforcement officer is justified in using reasonable force against another person to effect an arrest, or to prevent the other person's escape, if a felony has been committed, and the person has probable cause to believe the other person committed that felony.   However, the person is not justified in using deadly force unless authorized by the other deadly force provisions discussed above.[375]

IX.   Exceptions to Legal Justification to Use Force.

There are four necessary and logical exceptions to the statutory scheme authorizing the use of force to protect a person and/ or property based on the imminent use of force.[376]

First, a person is not legally justified in using force if he/she is committing, or escaping after the commission of, a crime.[377]

Second, the legal justification for the use of force is inapplicable to a person who provokes unlawful action by another person, with the intent to cause bodily injury to that other person.[378]

Third, no defense to the use of force will lie where a person has entered into combat with another person, or is the initial aggressor, unless the person withdraws from the encounter and communicates to the other person the intent to do so, and the other person nevertheless continues or threatens to continue unlawful action.[379]

Fourth, legal justification for force is inapplicable if a person continues to combat another person after the other person withdraws from the encounter and communicates the other person's intent to stop hijacking, attempting to hijack, or otherwise seizing or attempting to seize unlawful control of an aircraft in flight.[380]

X.   Crimes from Unjustified Use of Force.

A person who uses unjustified force causing death is subject to prosecution and potential conviction for murder,[381] voluntary manslaughter,[382] involuntary manslaughter,[383] or reckless homicide.[384] Injury, but not death, would subject the defendant to prosecution and potential conviction for battery,[385] aggravated battery,[386] domestic battery,[387] or criminal recklessness.[388]

XI.   Conclusion.

The use of force, particularly deadly force, is difficult to summarize. Literally, every use of force is different and the facts vary widely. The licensee must be fully advised of the statutory legal standards for the use of force, including deadly force, in order to follow the law, when and if such a situation should arise.

In no uncertain terms, the licensee should avoid any known or perceived scenario where such an issue may arise. In even the clearest case calling for the use of force, including deadly force, the licensee's life will change permanently in unimaginable ways.

In the author's opinion, the real power with this legal justification and affirmative defense extended to Indiana's citizenry is in the discretion to avoid use of deadly force.

129

130

Chapter 15

Response to the Use of Force

> "The art of war is of vital importance to the state. It is a matter of life and death, a road to safety or ruin. Hence under no circumstances can it be neglected."
> –Sun Tzu, The Art of War (circa, 500 B.C.)

I.   Introduction.

While it is hoped that any use of force, including deadly force, is so clear and the necessity of self-defense apparent, that no discussion is needed in this Book, this is often not the case. In fact, hundreds of Indiana cases demonstrate otherwise.[389]

What should be readily apparent by this juncture in the Book, is that many questions related to the use of force, turn on questions of detailed fact as applied to specific legal standards. Every case is different, and this is particularly true with deadly force cases.

Such factual variance, coupled with the tremendous consequence of force, especially deadly force, precludes any bright-line rules about what a person should do following the use of force.

What follows is a general protocol provided to inform the person about one of many legally proper ways to respond to the immediate aftermath of the use of deadly force. The sole purpose of this model is to help protect one's constitutional, and other rights, in the wholly confusing time immediately following a deadly force scenario. The objective is to properly position the licensee's case(s) for the future.

The discussion of this model gives way to a general analysis of what to initially expect and anticipate from a criminal and/or civil perspective following the deadly force event.

II. Protocol for Immediate Aftermath of Force.

There are immediate and appropriate actions to engage in following the use of deadly force. While seemingly common sense, the time immediately following a deadly force event is dangerous, chaotic, and confused.

The initial step is not thinking through whether the "right call" was made on the use of deadly force. There will be plenty of time for consideration of this later; and this event, specifically, will be played, and replayed, numerous times, on a variety of fronts, in the weeks, months, and years to follow. The proper immediate focus is to first reduce risk.

A. Risk Reduction.

The risk and danger following a deadly force encounter is multi-faceted. The person (who is now assumed to be a licensee for purposes of this analysis) must first assess his/her own safety and security, which is addressed by the following questions and their answers:

1.   Is the aggressor(s) still a risk to the licensee?

2.   Is the licensee at risk of harm from other sources?

3.   Are the weapons properly secured?

If the aggressor is still a risk and danger to the licensee, he/she should take actions to ensure safety without the use of additional force (such as flight, distance, barriers, etc.). If additional force is necessary, it must, as always, be the minimum amount of force.

Once the licensee has sufficiently reduced the risk from the aggressor to himself/herself, collateral risk sources must be considered. This would include a "good samaritan" without sufficient information, coming to the aid of the aggressor, through self-defense and the use of force against the licensee, or emergency personnel doing likewise.

Finally, a critical part of this risk reduction is placing the licensee's handgun (and any other weapons at the scene) in a place that is not only safe, but also non-threatening to the arriving first responders, such as police officers.

[!] **CAUTION, Being Perceived as a Threat to a First-Responder:** First-responders, such as law enforcement officers, have the unfortunate job of arriving at the scene of any deadly force event in its obvious state of confusion and chaos. The licensee must make sure that he/she is not displaying his/her firearm in any manner that might be perceived as aggressive.

B.   Aid for Aggressor.

Once the licensee's safety is ensured, the licensee must next take immediate action to aid the aggressor. This would include first aid to the best of his/her ability and training, within the bounds of safety, and/or summoning professional medical help.[390] Typically, this is done by and through a 911 call.

[!] CAUTION, Aiding the Aggressor: The licensee has a legal duty to aid the injured aggressor after he/she is removed from danger.

However, while the licensee must summon help, it is in the licensee's best interest to avoid making any admissions of any type. Emergency calls are recorded, and will be one piece of the evidence used in assessing the lawfulness of the use of the force.

C.   Invoke Silence and Counsel.

Even in the "cleanest" event of the use of deadly force from a legal perspective, there will be intense scrutiny of the matter later, as there should be. No matter how justified it may seem at the time, there are always a myriad of variables on which the legal tides may turn.

This stated, it is at this juncture that some readers of this Book will "cringe", particularly those in the law enforcement community. The third step is to exercise one's right to remain silent and to have legal counsel. This is a basic and fundamental constitutional right.[391]

The proper response to arriving first-responders questioning a licensee would be as follows: "Officer I want to fully assist you in your investigation, but I am going to invoke my right to silence and counsel, and I am not making any statements or comments, until I have spoken with an attorney."

[!] CAUTION, Do Not Make Statements: Despite a desire to explain the use of deadly force, do not. Period. Upon initial approach of the law enforcement officer, do not even posit that you discharged your firearm. Instead, reply, as previously indicated.

[!] CAUTION, Lawful Interview Tactics: The reader must be aware that it is constitutional for a law enforcement officer to make assertions that are false, or otherwise, to obtain a confession. This is their job. It is to catch the bad guy. Despite any apparent "deal" you are offered, promises made, or bleak picture painted, remain silent and obtain counsel.[392]

This third step is incredibly difficult. The desire to explain one's actions in such an event is, at times, overpowering. However, even assuming that the use of force was fully and totally justified (and as a general principle, this is never the case), tremendous value will be placed on initial statements.

Operating under the state of shock that comes with the surreal event of a shooting and the use of deadly force, is no time to make such a statement. The reader may be surprised to learn this, but false confessions through coercive police tactics are not necessarily uncommon.[393]

If the licensee is arrested (as opposed to released until review or screened by a prosecutor), the right to silence should continue and should be asserted, specifically, along with the right of counsel.

In any event, no matter how clear the case appears, the licensee must retain competent legal criminal defense counsel, and civil counsel, before taking any further action or making any statements.

III. Chronology of Deadly Force Case.

A. Criminal Component.

1. No Criminal Charge.

Depending upon whether facts tend to demonstrate the propriety of the use of deadly force, a person using deadly force may be allowed to leave until law enforcement and the prosecutor investigate and analyze the matter. In any event, depending on the facts, the prosecutor has the discretion to decide whether to criminally pursue the case. If the matter is a clear and legally justified use of deadly force, the prosecutor may exercise his/her discretion and not file charges.[394]

2. Grand Jury.

In closer calls, or those that have political overtones, where there are "camps" on both sides of the issue, the prosecutor may not charge the person, but instead present the matter to a grand jury. The purpose of a grand jury is to determine for the prosecutor if the person should be charged. If the person is indicted by the grand jury, the criminal case moves forward.[395]

3. Criminal Trial.

In the balance of cases, the person is arrested, charged, and bonds out pending a criminal trial, where the affirmative defense of self-defense will be asserted. If at trial the defendant is acquitted, the matter is over and he/she cannot be re-tried due to the double jeopardy provision of the U.S. Constitution.[396]

B.   Civil Component.

As a practical matter, even if the use of deadly force is clearly justified, it is almost a legal certainty that the licensee will be sued. The suit will be for wrongful death, or other negligent and/or intentional torts if the "victim" survives. This may seem illogical, but the author has been involved in many of these cases, and this is almost always the result.

The reason for the likelihood of being sued is because the burden of proof is lower in a civil case,[397] making the likelihood of winning higher. Further, there are often very high damages, thereby making the case financially attractive to a plaintiff's counsel. Furthermore, if the "victim" can allege negligence, then it is possible that insurance coverage may be available from which to recover.[398]

IV.   Conclusion.

Following a deadly force encounter, the first concern should be risk reduction, followed by aid for the aggressor, and invocation of the right to counsel and silence. Depending upon the facts of the case, the licensee may be charged or the case may be heard by a grand jury. In clear cases, the prosecutor may exercise his/her discretion and not charge any crime. Whatever the outcome of the force event and criminal prosecution, the licensee will most likely be sued for wrongful death and/or other torts. As such, defense counsel should be retained at once.

138

COMMON QUESTIONS & ANSWERS

> "'Question.' An interrogative expression often used to test knowledge."
> –Merriam Webster's Collegiate Dictionary (12th ed), p. 955

I.   General Questions.

Question #1:   Are there any reference guides to help me select a handgun for personal protection? *Answer:* Yes, there are several books.[399] *Discussion:* The author's personal opinion is that the "perfect" carry gun for self-defense for a novice is a .38 Special DAO revolver. This gun has a heavy trigger pull, and is absolutely reliable. The only malfunction conceivable is the "dumping" of the rounds. However, this is a very complex question on the whole, and requires careful research and consideration.

Question #2:   Are there any special resource materials available to women concerning carrying a handgun for self-defense? *Answer:* Yes. *Discussion:*   Perhaps the most well known author on issues of guns and self-defense, from the female perspective, is Paxton Quigley.[400]

Question #3:   Can I arrest another person with a citizen's arrest? *Answer:* Yes. *Discussion:*   The authority to perform a citizen's arrest is by statute. This statute allows any person to arrest another person in one of three circumstances: (1) if the person to be arrested committed a felony in the citizen's presence; (2) if a felony has been committed, and the citizen has probable cause to believe that the other person committed that felony; or (3) if a breach of the peace is being committed in the citizen's presence, and the arrest is necessary to prevent the continuance of the breach of the peace.

This area of law is relatively undeveloped. Furthermore, any citizen performing such an arrest would have no civil or criminal immunity from prosecution in association therewith. This area is rife with risk, and any citizen performing a citizen's arrest, had better be sure of the lawful basis for such an arrest.[401]

Question #4: **Is there any type of custom work I should not have done to the handgun I carry for self-defense?** *Answer:* Yes. *Discussion:* Any work that could reduce the weapon's reliability or accuracy, although these are generally the opposite characteristics of what custom work attempts to achieve. The most significant area of custom work to be avoided is any work to change and lighten the trigger pull. A heavy trigger pull is typically a standard criterion of a proper self-defense pistol, and reducing the pull weight, may lead to an accidental discharge in the stress of a deadly force situation.

Question #5: **What do I do if I am unsure if licensed carry is legal and permissible in a given place and context?** *Answer:* Do not carry. *Discussion:* As noted throughout this Book, there are several questionable areas of carry under state and federal law. This, coupled with our society's limited tolerance of breaches of safety and security issues post-September 11, 2001, simply makes the risk of improper carry, arrest, prosecution, and conviction too great. Most of these crimes have substantial prison sentences associated with them.[402] However, it is anticipated that several of these ambiguous areas of the law will be clarified over the next few years, further allowing the licensee to have defined carry boundaries.

Question #6: **Are there national trends on gun laws that I might expect to see proposed and/or passed into law in Indiana in the future?** *Answer:* Yes. *Discussion:* Laws enacted in other states often provide an excellent precursor of what might be expected to be proposed and ultimately enacted into law in Indiana. Substantial restrictions found in other states that are unlike those in Indiana are preclusions of carry at taverns, state/local government buildings/property, and major public events.[403] Also, from a federal perspective, it is anticipated that substantial additional laws, rules, and regulations regarding mass transportation will be enacted by the TSA and/or the Congress.

Question #7: **Can I mail my handgun through the United States Post Office for work or repairs as long as it is shipped to another licensed dealer?** *Answer:* No. *Discussion:* The rules and regulations of the USPS preclude this.[404] Private carriers may be used, but they have specific requirements regarding shipping firearms, and must be consulted in advance.

Question #8: **What do I do if I am in another state and find a handgun I want to purchase?** *Answer:* As a general matter, this cannot be done. *Discussion:* A person may be able to legally arrange for a Federal Firearms License holder in their state to purchase the weapon, have it shipped to his/her store, and then sell it to the licensee upon return to Indiana.

Question #9: **Are there any special laws on children and handguns?** *Answer:* Yes. *Discussion:* The article on weapons in the Indiana penal code has an entire chapter addressing children and handguns/firearms. This provision of the code has criminal implications for a child and/or parent of a child possessing and/or using a firearm for any illicit purpose. While discussion of this is beyond the scope of this Book, a parent and/or child faced with a child handling firearms should be familiar with these laws. Generally, these criminal laws do not apply to a (1) child in a hunters or firearms safety course; (2) supervised child target practicing; (3)

child engaged in included competition shooting; (4) child hunting or trapping with a valid license; (5) child traveling to an approved activity with an unloaded firearm; (6) child on the property of family and with permission to possess the firearm; and (7) child who is at his/her residence and has permission from his/her parent to possess the firearm.[405]

Question #10: **Are there any special considerations if I carry my handgun in the scope of my employment?** *Answer:* Yes. *Discussion:* The first consideration is if the Superintendent has enacted any administrative rules regarding carry within the scope of the licensee's employment.[406]   Second, the licensee should inquire about the employer's specific policies and rules and regulations. Third, the licensee must determine if acts of deadly force will be covered by the employer insofar as a criminal and/or civil defense is concerned. The licensee may be surprised to learn that this is often not the case.

Question #11: **What do I do if my handgun is stolen?** *Answer:* Make a police report. *Discussion:* The reason for this is obvious. What if the weapon winds up at a crime scene? Through the "paper trail" associated with modern handgun sales, a weapon can be traced back to the factory through firearms dealers' logs and ATF 4473 forms.[407]

Question #12: **Will I have liability if my gun is used to perpetrate a crime?** *Answer:* Maybe. Indiana law is in a great state of flux on this issue as of the time of the publication of this Book. *Discussion:* In July, 2003, the Indiana Supreme Court held a duty exists to exercise reasonable and ordinary care in the storage and safekeeping of firearms.[408]   However, in response, legislation was proposed in the General Assembly providing wide immunity from civil liability for firearms used in the commission of crimes[409].

Question #13: Do Indiana residents have the right to keep and bear arms? *Answer:* Yes. *Discussion:* Article I § 32 of the Indiana Constitution guarantees the right to keep and bear arms.[410]

II.   Considerations and Restrictions on Firearms and Ammunition.

Question #14: Can the sale of firearms be suspended during an emergency/disaster? *Answer:* Yes.[411] *Discussion:* In the event of a qualifying disaster,[412] a legislative body of a governmental unit,[413] or if the legislative body cannot be convened due to the emergency, the executive of the municipality,[414] may adopt an emergency ordinance suspending the sale of firearms for up to seventy-two hours.[415]

Question #15: Can the Legislature enact laws limiting my constitutional gun rights? *Answer:* Yes. *Discussion:* The Courts have consistently ruled that the Legislature has the power to enact reasonable regulations for the use and possession of firearms, particularly handguns.[416]

Question #16:   Are there any restrictions on the types of ammunition I may possess and/or use in my handgun? *Answer:* Yes.   *Discussion:* This limitation is both state and federal in nature. Specifically, under Indiana law, a person may not possess armor-piercing handgun ammunition, which has been defined as a cartridge that can be fired from a handgun that will, upon firing, expel a projectile that has a metal core and outer coating of plastic.[417] Further, as a matter of federal law, any criminal act committed with armor-piercing handgun ammunition is enhanced.[418] Also, a person may not manufacture or import armor piercing ammunition.[419] Under federal law armor-piercing ammunition is ammunition manufactured with a projectile, or projectile core, that is constructed entirely from one, or a combination of, the following: tungsten alloys, steel, iron, brass, bronze, beryllium copper, or depleted uranium.[420]

Question #17:   Is the type of ammunition I use for self-defense of any importance? *Answer:* Yes. *Discussion:*   This is an extremely complex question and should be discussed by the licensee with a person knowledgeable in the field. Two points are important to note. First, do not use any handloads, custom, or non-standard ammunition for self-defense. This may later be used negatively in a criminal and/ or civil prosecution. Second, use ammunition specifically designed for self-defense. Without getting to the technical facets of ballistics, defensive ammunition is designed to expend its energy in a relatively short amount of matter, thus preventing over-penetration. Do not use "ball" ammo for self-defense.

Question #18:   Is state preemption of firearms law important? *Answer:* Yes   *Discussion:* State preemption of a legal area means that the laws of the given area can only be enacted by its legislature. This is quite significant regarding handgun law, because without preemption, the various counties and smaller political subdivisions may pass firearms laws, making compliance very difficult. The Legislature has preempted this area in Indiana. Thus, there is little local regulation of firearms.[421] There are two exceptions. The first is a qualified emergency allowing gun sales to be suspended for seventy-two hours.[422] The second allows local municipalities to enact rules and regulations on land, buildings, or other property owned or administered by the local government.[423] As a practical matter, there are limited reference compilations of such rules and regulations. The licensee facing this issue should contact the building superintendent or building authority of such property to investigate the matter. (*See* Indianapolis-Marion County Building Authority Rules and Regulations Governing City-County Building and Grounds at Appendix "7", for a local government rule based on this statute).

III.   Licensing Questions.

Question #19: **Can I carry a handgun without a license?** *Answer:* Yes, in certain specific and narrowly defined places. *Discussion:* The licensing statute allows for the carry and/or possession of a handgun without a license in one's dwelling and property or fixed place of business. However, carrying is broadly construed, and the locations are narrowly defined or are undefined. A person seeking to carry under these exceptions must understand them fully in order to comply with the law and avoid arrest, prosecution, and conviction for carrying a handgun without a license.[424]

Question #20: **Are there different types of handgun licenses that are available to Indiana residents?** *Answer:* Yes. *Discussion:* There are two types of permits for carry authorized by the Legislature. The first is for protection of person and property, which is called an unlimited permit. The second is a qualified license for hunting and target practice only. The application criteria is the same for both licenses. The only difference between these licenses, other than permissible places of carry, is the cost of the license.[425]

Question #21: **Is there a cost for a handgun license?** *Answer:* Yes. *Discussion:*   There is a ten dollar application processing fee, five dollars of which is to be refunded by the local police processing agency if the permit is not issued by the Superintendent. Additionally, there is a five dollar fee for a qualified license and a fifteen dollar license fee for an unlimited license.[426]

Question #22: **Is there a certain place I should go to obtain an Indiana handgun application for a license?** *Answer:* Yes. *Discussion:* A person desiring to become a licensee should contact the chief of police, or corresponding law enforcement officer, of the municipality in which the applicant resides to obtain the application. If the municipality has no such officer, or the applicant does not live within a city or town, then he/she makes application to the county sheriff.[427]

Question #23: **Can my local police department refuse to provide me with an application for a handgun license?** *Answer:* No. *Discussion:* This issue has long been decided. The City of Gary, Indiana, tried to do this effective January 1, 1980. Ultimately, the Indiana Supreme Court held that the Gary citizens, denied an application by the police department, could bring a civil rights action against the City of Gary.[428]

Question #24: **If I lose my handgun license, can I obtain a replacement?** *Answer:* Yes. *Discussion:* Replacement licenses are available for a fee of five dollars.[429] As a practical matter, given the rise in identity theft, and the inherent power of a handgun license in the wrong person's possession, the licensee should take great care to ensure that the license is not lost.

Question #25: **Can I transport my handgun without a license?** *Answer:* Yes, in certain circumstances. *Discussion:* If the handgun is in a secure wrapper, and unloaded, a person may transport his/her handgun from the place of purchase to his dwelling and property or fixed place of business, or to a place of repair or back to his/her dwelling or fixed place of business, or in moving from one dwelling or business to another.[430]

Question #26: **Does a handgun license expire?** *Answer:* Yes. *Discussion:* A handgun license is valid for a period of four years, whether qualified or unqualified, unless suspended or revoked. If the licensee applies for a renewal license within thirty days of expiration of the license, the license is automatically extended as valid until passage by the Superintendent on the renewal application.[431]

IV. Carry Questions.

Question #27: **Is my handgun license valid for carry in other states?** *Answer:* Yes, in states that have passed reciprocal laws. *Discussion:* However, this right only enures to the Indiana licensee by the statutes of other states. As such, an Indiana license is not recognized in all states. Further, in those states that do recognize Indiana's permits, the licensee is bound by all handgun laws of the reciprocal state, which may differ substantially from Indiana law.[432]

Question #28: **With an Indiana handgun license, can I carry my handgun in all places throughout the state?** *Answer:* No. *Discussion:* There are several areas of limitation applicable to an unlimited license holder.   Major state exceptions include penal and juvenile facilities, schools, and airports and airplanes. Two federal exceptions are quite broad. The first provides that a handgun cannot be carried onto any federal property staffed by federal employees, except for permitted hunting.[433]   Additionally, weapons of all types may be prohibited from mass transportation facilities and vehicles.[434]

Question #29: Does my handgun license allow me to carry my handgun to work? *Answer:* Probably not. *Discussion:* Under Indiana law, property owners and lessees have great authority regarding ability to regulate affairs on their property. The interest holder (an employer) of private property has the inherent authority to make rules and regulations applying to employees and visitors on the property, which may preclude the carrying of a handgun. Violation would subject the employee to termination and expulsion from the property. Failure to leave upon request by the owner may constitute criminal trespass. Thus, the employee must understand his/her company's position on this. Many employers preclude carry of a handgun at work due to liability and insurance considerations.[435]

Question #30: Must I tell a police officer that I have a handgun with me in my vehicle, if pulled over for a traffic stop? *Answer:* You should, although it is not a provision of the Indiana licensing statutes.[436] *Discussion:* Many states require this by law and/or as a condition of handgun licensing. Non-disclosure could easily lead to a situation where in trying to obtain information for the police officer, the gun becomes exposed, and the officer believes the motorist is trying to obtain the weapon for criminal purposes. Thus, the proper protocol in any traffic stop is to roll down the window and place one's hands on the windowsill, in plain view of the officer, and immediately inform the officer of the possession of the weapon.

Question #31: Can I carry my handgun into special events and venues? *Answer:* Most likely, no. *Discussion:* Most venues clearly prohibit handguns even with a license. The license does not supersede a property interest holder's right to restrict weapons on their property. As a practical matter, many venues search patrons, and bar those with a weapon from entry. If one is caught in possession of a handgun after entry, expulsion is standard operating procedure.[437]

Question #32: **Can I carry my handgun into a public place where "no handguns" signage is posted?** *Answer:* No. *Discussion:* A private property owner has the right to restrict or prohibit handguns on the property. Failure to adhere to their conditions of entry onto the land can result in the property owner requesting the licensee to leave, and failure to do so may constitute criminal trespass.

Question #33: **Can I enact restrictions on handgun possession on my private property?** *Answer:* Yes. *Discussion:* Again, as noted, a private property owner has vast rights to control his/her property. This includes the right to regulate those entering the property with handguns. While failure of the guest to follow any private rules and regulations regarding handguns would not result in a criminal act (in Indiana), it would subject the guest to being ejected from the property. Failure to leave would then constitute criminal and civil trespass.[438]

Question #34: **Can I carry my handgun and other guns to foreign countries?** *Answer:* In some cases. *Discussion:* Typically, this question is posed by those wanting to travel overseas on a hunting excursion. The guide or organization sponsoring the hunt should provide this information. However, as a general rule, any "military style" weapons are prohibited. Furthermore, the weapons must be transported in the cargo hold of the aircraft and appropriately secured. The airlines should be consulted with regard to their policies and procedures. This is relatively easy as such information is typically on the respective airlines website (as is the case with other forms of transportation).

Question #35: **Do I have to carry my handgun concealed with my Indiana license?** *Answer:* You should. *Discussion:* The licensing statute does not require concealed carry.[439]   However, many states do require this by statute, while other states allow open carry. Short of carrying in the scope of employment for deterrence purposes, or during hunting, open carry negates most tactical, self-defense aspects of carry.

Question #36:   **Are there any special considerations of carry of a handgun for hunters using a handgun for lawful hunting?** *Answer:* Yes. *Discussion:* Pursuant to administrative rules adopted by the Natural Resources Commission, there are several limitations with handgun hunting. Several of the broad restrictions are noted in this question, but the administrative code must be consulted for specific, complete information.   These exceptions largely regard deer hunting. First, the handgun (1) must conform to the handgun regulation requirements of the criminal code; (2) have a barrel of at least four inches; and (3) fire a bullet of .243 inch diameter or larger. Second, the handgun must not be carried concealed. Third, full metal jacket bullets are unlawful. Fourth, the handgun must be unloaded in the field outside of lawful hunting hours. Finally, all 25/20, 32/20, 30 carbine, and 38 special ammunition is prohibited.[440]

Question #37:   **Is my handgun license restricted to a certain carry handgun?** *Answer:* No. *Discussion:* It allows the licensee to carry any handgun he/she lawfully possesses. It is not gun specific. However, for purposes of carry for self-defense, varying weapon type is typically a bad idea. Complete familiarity with the carry weapon is critical. For example, the author represented a client in a case properly involving the use of deadly force, in which the lack of familiarity with the weapon directly resulted in a "stove-pipe" on the first shot, thereby rendering the weapon useless.

Question #38: Can I carry more than one handgun at a time

with a handgun license? *Answer:* Yes. *Discussion:* Aside from possession of multiple guns for going to the range, this question generally arises in the context of a licensee wanting to carry a primary and backup gun. There are many schools of thought on this issue. For police officers, it is a must. For the typical licensee carrying for self-defense, this is a personal choice. However, it doubles the weapons one must be familiar with, practiced with, and maintain. This author believes that in most circumstances, the money paid for two guns would be better spent buying a "better" or "higher quality" single gun. The average licensee is unlikely to be proficient enough to properly transition to a secondary gun. If anything, the licensee would be better served carrying a spare magazine or speed loader in lieu of a second weapon.

Question #39: **Do I have to keep my license with me if I am carrying a handgun?** *Answer:* Yes. *Discussion:* Outside of the specific, statutory places, namely one's dwelling or property/fixed place of business, a handgun license and possession thereof is required to carry a handgun. Furthermore, a license is not an element of the crime of carrying a handgun without a license. A person found with a handgun who does not have his/her handgun license in possession, would be subject to arrest and prosecution. The burden to prove the existence of a valid handgun license would be on the licensee.[441]

Question #40: **Is there any type of handgun I should not carry for self-defense?** *Answer:* Yes. *Discussion:* Again this is very complex question with a myriad of variables. However, big bore magnums (.44 and .357) and "military style" pistols should be avoided due to the typical perception of jurors, judges, and prosecutors. Further, magnums may be too powerful and large for practical carry for self-defense. Finally, the weapon must not be so small of a caliber, or of such poor quality, that it cannot meet its self-defense role.

V.   Criminal Acts and Handguns.

Question #41:   **Can I still carry my handgun if I have a protective order, restraining order, or no contact order against me?** *Answer:* Most likely, no. *Discussion:* Any court issuing a qualifying order will notify the Superintendent. (*See* Appendix "8" for the Indiana-approved notice form the court sends to the Indiana State Police Superintendent). The Superintendent then suspends the license. Furthermore, once the licensee has notice of the order, it is a federal crime to purchase, receive, or possess a firearm.[442]

Question #42:   **Are there crimes and/or other circumstances that totally preclude possession of a handgun?** *Answer:* Yes. *Discussion:* There are many such circumstances. Three common examples are: (1) a person with a conviction for domestic battery;[443] (2) a person that is classified as a serious violent felon;[444] or (3) a person on probation.

Question #43: **Can I brandish my handgun to scare off someone?** *Answer:* No. *Discussion:* A person who knowingly or intentionally points a firearm at another person commits a Class D felony. However, the offense is a Class A misdemeanor if the firearm was not loaded.[445]

VI.   Use of Force.

Question #44: Can I use deadly force in Indiana? *Answer:* Yes, in certain narrowly defined contexts, although prudent measures should prevent a licensee from ever being in any such situation. *Discussion:* The legal justification for the use of deadly force is codified. First, a person may use force, including deadly force, only if he/she reasonably believes that such force is necessary to prevent death or serious bodily injury to himself/herself, a third party, or to stop a forcible felony.[446] Second, a licensee may use reasonable force, including deadly force, if the person reasonably believes that the force is necessary to prevent or terminate the other person's unlawful entry of or attack on the licensee's dwelling or curtilage.[447] Third, force, including deadly force, is justified against another person if such force is necessary to prevent or stop a hijacking of an aircraft while in flight in Indiana.[448]

Question #45: **Is there any particular protocol I should follow if I use deadly force?** *Answer:* Yes. *Discussion:* Determine if the aggressor still poses a risk of harm, or if there is harm posed from other sources. Secure all weapons known in a safe situation that is not a threat to any first-responder, and aid the aggressor. Then remain silent and retain counsel. This is your constitutional right. If questioned by police officers, respond as follows: "Officer, I am invoking my right to counsel and to remain silent."

Question #46: **I have heard that if I use deadly force outside, I should drag the person back inside my home?** *Answer:* No. *Discussion:* This belief likely hinges on the inherent notion that "a man's home is his castle," and can be protected inside with deadly force. However, with modern forensic science, the crime scene can be carefully and fully determined. It may even be a crime to interfere with the crime scene in this way.[449]

Question #47: **Will my homeowner's insurance cover my criminal and/or civil defense if I am prosecuted and/or sued for**

the use of deadly force? *Answer:* Most likely, no. ***Discussion:*** A typical homeowner's policy excludes intentional acts. Self-defense by definition is an intentional act, even if justified. However, it is possible that the broader coverage of an umbrella policy may pay for at least the defense cost of an attorney. However, it is very likely that even if the policy holder asserts a claim for a defense, that the insurance company will seek a declaratory judgment action to determine the act is beyond the scope of the insurance.[450]

Question #48: **Will my gun be confiscated if I use deadly force?** *Answer:* Yes. ***Discussion:*** It is standard operating procedure to confiscate the weapon and maintain it in the police impound/property room. Ultimately, if the use of force is determined to be justified, then the weapon may be returned to the owner. Typically, with the decision not to charge, the defendant's lawyer may be able to seek release by agreement of the prosecutor. In other cases, such as acquittal or dismissal of a filed case, the Court may order release. (*See* Appendix "9" for an actual Motion to Release Handgun and Order Granting Motion to Release Handgun utilized by the author). There is much variance on this position among the Indiana trial courts.

Question #49: **Will I be arrested if I use deadly force?** *Answer:* It depends. ***Discussion:*** The police officers at the scene typically make this call in conjunction with the prosecutor on call if this is after hours. Remember, no matter what, do not make any statements, and retain competent counsel.[451]

Appendix   1

Indiana Application for Handgun License

<table>
<tr><td colspan="2">

APPLICATION FOR HANDGUN LICENSE

State Form 36991 (R9/5-99)   No. 1302

Approved by State Board of Accounts 1974

</td><td>

State o

ORI - _____

County of _____

</td><td>

No.

</td></tr>
</table>

INSTRUCTIONS: I   All questions must be answered (type ████████)
    I   INDIANA STATE POLICE NOT RESPONSIBLE FOR INCORRECT OR ILLEGIBLE APPLICATION.
    I   PLEASE DO NOT SEND CASH: Postal Money Order or Certified Check in the correct amount, made payable to the STATE OF INDIANA must accompany this application. PERSONAL CHECKS NOT ACCEPTED and will be returned.

NOTE: Any person giving false information or offering false evidence to obtain a firearm license shall be deemed guilty of a felony and upon conviction may be punished by imprisonment for five (5) years to which may be added a fine of not more than $10,000.

I understand that if a license is granted I may carry any handgun or handguns lawfully possessed.

To the Superintendent of the Indiana State Police:

Date (month, day, year)

I, _____ do hereby make application for a license to have in my possession and carry on my person or in my vehicle, any handgun with a barrel less than sixteen (16) inches in length or any firearm with an overall length of less than twenty-six (26) inches. Subject to the laws of the State of Indiana.

Name (first, middle, last)			Date of birth (mo., day, yr.)				Nationality	
Address (street number or R.R.)			Place of birth				Citizenship	
City, state and ZIP code			Age	Race	Sex		Height	Weight
My residence is located within the city or town limits of: IN Initial _____			Build	Hair	Color of eyes		Scars and marks	
My residence is NOT located within the limits of any city or town: Initial _____	How long have you been a resident of Indiana? From: To:							
Occupation	Have you previously held an Indiana Handgun License? ☐ Yes ☐ No		If Yes, year		License number			
Business address (street number or R.R.)	Has your Handgun license ever been suspended or revoked? ☐ Yes ☐ No		If Yes, date (year) suspended					
City, state, ZIP code	If Yes, reason suspended							
Have you ever been convicted of ANY CRIMINAL violation including DUI? ☐ Yes ☐ No	If Yes, state charges							
Have you ever been treated for psychiatric health care of an emotional or mental illness? ☐ Yes ☐ No	If Yes, (a) list year of recent treatment, and		(b) submit documentation/recommendation from treating Mental Health Professional or Treatment Center.					

I desire a license for the purpose of: (check only one)	Signature of applicant	
☐ (1) Hunting and/or Target Practice -- Fee $5.00		
☐ (2) Personal Protection -- Fee $15.00	Subscribed and sworn to before me this _____ day of _____, _____.	**NOTARY SEAL**
☐ (3) Firearm Dealer -- Fee Exempt	Signature of Notary Public	
☐ (4) Retired Police officer -- Fee Exempt	My commission expires	City	County

THIS APPLICATION MUST BE FILLED IN COMPLETELY AND ALL QUESTIONS ANSWERED

DISTRIBUTION: This copy to be forwarded to the Superintendent, Indiana State Police, Indiana Government Center North, 100 North Senate Avenue, Room 302, Indianapolis, IN 46204-2259.

Indiana Handgun Law, 2005

Appendix 2

IPD/MCSD Instruction Sheet for Application

INSTRUCTIONS TO APPLY FOR A PERSONAL PROTECTION FIREARMS PERMIT THROUGH THE INDIANAPOLIS POLICE DEPARTMENT OR THE MARION COUNTY SHERIFF'S DEPARTMENT

- APPLICATION PROCEDURE -

- Please read these instructions and the application for handgun license completely and carefully.

- Insure your application is *typed*, *notarized*, *all questions have been answered* and *the application is completed*.

- If applicable, do not fail to admit your <u>full</u> arrest record. Failure to comply may lead to denial of a license.

- Submit a $15.00 money order or certified check made payable to the **State of Indiana** (*personal checks are not acceptable*). Your money order <u>must</u> accompany the application.

  In addition, a $10.00 application fee is to be paid at the time the application is submitted. The application fee must be paid in cash.

- Bring the completed documents, money order or certified check and application fee to the:

  Indianapolis Police Department Citizens Service Desk
  Room E100, 50 N. Alabama Street
  Indianapolis, Indiana

  Hours of Operation are 8:00 A.M to 4:00 P.M Monday through Friday (excepting national holidays).

- You will be notified by mail as to the approval or denial of your handgun license.

- SPECIAL NOTICE -

ALL QUESTIONS MUST BE ANSWERED TRUTHFULLY AND COMPLETELY. ANY FAILURE TO COMPLY WITH THE REQUIREMENTS OF THE INDIANAPOLIS POLICE DEPARTMENT AND/OR THE INDIANA STATE POLICE ON THE APPLICATION MAY RESULT IN THE DENIAL OF YOUR HANDGUN LICENSE.

IPD Form 3-4-50 R9

Appendix 3

Indiana License to Carry Handgun

Appendix   4

Superintendent's Letter of Suspension

STATE OF INDIANA

INDIANA STATE POLICE

INDIANA GOVERNMENT CENTER NORTH
100 NORTH SENATE AVENUE

INDIANAPOLIS, INDIANA   46204-2259
www.state.in.us/isp

February ▆▆▆▆ .
File No: ▆▆▆▆▆▆

Dear ▆▆▆▆▆▆

Information has been received by the Superintendent of the Indiana State Police Department which gives reasonable grounds to believe that you are not a "Proper person" to retain your license to carry a handgun, specifically:

240 IAC 3-1-1. ISSUANCE; IMPROPER PERSONS; RESTRICTED LICENSES:

SEC. 1 ISSUANCE. (1) The Superintendent of the Indiana State Police Department will not issue a firearm license which would place a licensee in contradiction of Federal Firearm Law. Under 18 United States Code Section 922.

   (n) It shall be unlawful for any person who is under indictment for a crime punishable by imprisonment for a term exceeding one year to ship or transport in interstate or foreign commerce any firearm or ammunition or receive any firearm or ammunition which has been shipped or transported in interstate or foreign commerce; and

   (g) It shall be unlawful for any person—

   (8) Who is subject to a court order that—

      (A) Was issued after a hearing of which such person received actual notice, and at which such person had the opportunity to participate;
      (B) restrains such person from harassing, stalking, or threatening an intimate partner or person or child of such intimate partner or person, or engaging in other conduct that would place an intimate partner in reasonable fear of bodily injury to the partner or child; and
      (C) (i) includes a finding that such person represents a credible threat to the physical safety of such intimate partner or child; or
      (ii) by its terms explicitly prohibits the use, attempted use, or threatened use of physical force against such intimate partner or child that would reasonably be expected to cause bodily injury.

      ….to receive any firearm or ammunition which has shipped or transported in interstate or foreign commerce.

      (32) The term "intimate partner" means, with respect to a person, the spouse of the person, former spouse of the person, an individual who is a parent of a child of the person, and an individual who cohabitates or has cohabitated with the person.

INTEGRITY · SERVICE · PROFESSIONALISM

Therefore, it is ORDERED by the Superintendent, under the authority of I.C. 35-47-2-5, 240 IAC 3-2-1, that the license issued to you is hereby **SUSPENDED**, pending a hearing to be held on ████████ at the hour of ████████ , Indiana State Police Conference Room, Room 335, Indiana Government Center North, Indianapolis, Indiana. You are advised that you may be represented by counsel and may present evidence in your own behalf.

If you fail to attend or participate in the hearing, the Administrative Law Judge may determine that you are in default, that you have waived any right to further review for handgun licensing, and that the proceedings may be dismissed. For your information, you may contact the Administrative Law Judge or Agency Counsel at the following:

Major ████████
Administrative Law Judge
Indiana Government Center North
100 North Senate Avenue
Indianapolis, Indiana 46204
Telephone Number: ████████

Major ████████
Agency Counsel
████████
████████
Telephone Number: ████████

Any questions may be directed to ████████ Firearms Section, 317-████████

Sincerely,

Melvin J. Carraway
Superintendent

MJC:bsg
cc: ████████
cc: Bryan Ciyou, Attorney

Certified Mail No. ████████

Appendix   5

Superintendent's Letter of Reinstatement

STATE OF INDIANA

INDIANA STATE POLICE

INDIANA GOVERNMENT CENTER NORTH
100 NORTH SENATE AVENUE

INDIANAPOLIS, INDIANA   46204-2259
www.state.in.us/isp

December ▮▮▮▮▮

Our File: ▮▮▮▮▮▮

▮▮▮▮▮▮
▮▮▮▮▮▮
▮▮▮▮▮▮

Dear Mr. ▮▮▮▮

Regarding the Administrative Hearing and suspension of Indiana Handgun License ▮▮▮▮▮ The hearing was held on ▮▮▮▮▮▮, whereas you were found in **Default** and the license **Revoked** under IC 35-47-2-3-(g)-(4) has been arrested for a Class A or Class B felony, or any other felony that was committed while armed with a deadly weapon or that involved the use of violence, if a court has found probable cause to believe that the person committed the offense charged; and under 18 United State Code Section 922. (n) It shall be unlawful for any person who is under indictment for a crime punishable by imprisonment for a term exceeding one year.

Our Department has been provided with information from attorney Bryan L. Ciyou that shows the case pending has been expunged and after further review the revocation order issued has been **DISMISSED** and the license **REINSTATED.**

Sincerely,

Melvin J. Carraway
Superintendent

MJC:tel

cc: ▮▮▮▮▮▮

Certified Mail No.: ▮▮▮▮▮▮

INTEGRITY • SERVICE • PROFESSIONALISM

Appendix   6

Court Order on Firearms and Weapons

STATE OF INDIANA   )   IN THE MARION COUNTY CIRCUIT COURT
)SS:
COUNTY OF MARION   )

MAY 1 0 1999

ORDER ON FIREARMS AND WEAPONS

The Executive Committee of the Marion Superior Court
and the Judge of the Marion Circuit Court desire to provide
a safe environment for employees and the public visiting the
court facilities. In order to provide this safe environment
it is necessary to restrict the carrying of firearms and
weapons in and around any court facility or ancillary
agencies within the City-County Building.

IT IS THEREFORE ORDERED that firearms and weapons are
prohibited in and around any court facility or ancillary
agencies within the City-County Building by persons other
than police officers in uniform or displaying a police
issued ID. Additionally, persons wishing to enter the lower
level of the Center Tower or the West Wing of the City-
County Building shall consent to a screening of their person
and items in their possession by representatives of the
Marion County Sheriff. Persons failing to comply will be
denied entry.

IT IS FURTHER ORDERED that any police officer who is a
party to a case pending in Marion Superior Court or the
Marion Circuit Court shall not be allowed to bring a firearm

or weapon into the lower level of the Center Tower or the West Wing of the City-County Building.

IT IS FURTHER ORDERED that any firearm or weapon found may be confiscated and not returned. Weapons include, but are not limited to:

Guns of any kind	Scissors
Screwdrivers	Knives (pocket or otherwise)
Box cutters	Mace
Stereo equipment	Explosives

Or any item that could be used as a weapon or any item that could conceal a weapon.

Any person found in possession of a firearm without a valid license shall be subject to arrest pursuant to I.C. 35-47-2-1.

SO ORDERED this _____ day of May, 1999.

_____
Marion County Circuit Court

_____
Presiding Judge

_____
Assoc. Presiding Judge

_____
Assoc. Presiding Judge

E.O. 99-009

Appendix 7

County Government Rule on Weapons

INDIANAPOLIS-MARION COUNTY BUILDING AUTHORITY
Rules and Regulations Governing
The City-County Building and Grounds

1. **AUTHORITY.** These rules and regulations are promulgated pursuant to Chapter 54 of the Acts of the Indiana General Assembly for the year 1953, as amended; and the City-County Building Lease dated August 2, 1959, as approved by the City of Indianapolis and the Board of Commissioners of the County of Marion.

2. **APPLICABILITY.** These rules and regulations apply to the City-County Building and properties managed by and under the control of the Indianapolis-Marion County Building Authority, and to all persons entering in or on such properties. Each occupant tenant shall be responsible for the observance of these rules and regulations.

3. **RECORDING PRESENCE.** Except as otherwise ordered, the Building shall be closed to the public after normal working hours. The Building shall also be closed to the public in emergency situations and at such other times as may be necessary for the orderly conduct of the tenants' business. Admission to the Building during periods when it is closed to the public will be limited to authorized individuals who will be required to sign the register and/or display identification documents when requested by the Security Officer or other authorized individuals.

4. **PRESERVATION OF THE BUILDING.** The improper disposal of rubbish in the Building, spitting on property, creation of any hazard to persons or things, throwing of articles of any kind from the building, climbing upon the roof or any part of the Building, or the willful destruction, damage, or removal of property or any part thereof from the Building is prohibited.

5. **CONFORMITY WITH SIGNS AND EMERGENCY DIRECTIONS.** Persons in and about the Building shall comply with official signs of a prohibitory or directive nature, and during emergencies, with the direction of authorized individuals.

6. **DISTURBANCES.** Disorderly conduct in or about the Building, or conduct which creates loud and unusual or offensive noise, or which obstructs the usual use of entrances, foyers, corridors, offices, elevators, stairways, and parking lots, or which otherwise tends to impede or hinder public employees in the performance of their duties, or which impedes or hinders the general public from obtaining the services provided in the Building is prohibited. The occupant agency involved in a disturbance shall have initial responsibility for coordinating the observance of this rule by the public. Shirts and shoes must be worn at all times within the building. Indecent attire is prohibited.

7. **GAMBLING.** Participating in games for money or other personal property, or in the operating of gambling devices, the conduct of a lottery or pool, or the selling or purchasing of numbers or tickets, in or about the Building is prohibited.

8. **ALCOHOLIC BEVERAGES AND NARCOTICS.** Entering the Building, or operating a motor vehicle in the Building, by a person under the influence of alcoholic beverages or narcotic drugs is prohibited. The possession of alcoholic beverages in or about the Building is prohibited.

9. **SOLICITING, VENDING, AND DEBT COLLECTION.** Soliciting gifts or contributions of any kind, commercial soliciting and unapproved vending of all kinds, display or distribution of commercial advertising, or collecting private debts in or about the Building is prohibited.

10. **FOOD AND DRINKS.** Eating and drinking in the lobbies, corridors, and those areas not designated as eating areas is prohibited.

Date: November, 1995

11. **DISTRIBUTION OF HANDBILLS.** The distribution of material such as pamphlets, handbills, and flyers is prohibited without prior approval of an authorized official of the agency occupying the space where the material is to be distributed and the Building Authority.

12. **PHOTOGRAPHS FOR NEWS, ADVERTISING OR COMMERCIAL PURPOSES.** Photographs for news, advertising, or commercial purposes may be taken in space occupied by a tenant agency only with the consent of the occupying agency concerned. Except where security regulations apply, or court order or rule prohibits it, photographs for news purposes may be taken in entrances, lobbies, foyers, corridors or auditoriums when used for public meetings. Subject to the foregoing prohibitions, photographs for advertising and commercial purposes may be taken only with written permission of an authorized official of the agency occupying the space where the photographs are to be taken.

13. **USE OF COMMON AREAS.** Use of the common areas of the City-County Building including lobbies, corridors, the Public Assembly Room, Observatory, and other meeting rooms (generally those public areas not leased to governmental tenants) is restricted to the Building Authority and its governmental tenants. No displays, signs or other structures shall be erected in the common areas by any non-governmental, private group or individual since such objects may interfere with unobstructed and safe ingress and egress by employees of the governmental tenants and by the general public conducting business with government offices and courts in the City-County Building.

14. **USE OF COMMON AREAS FOR POLITICAL ACTIVITIES.** Use of the common areas of the City-County Building (generally those public areas not leased to the governmental tenants) for political activities is prohibited. No political signs, pictures or other materials shall be posted or displayed in common areas.

15. **DOGS AND OTHER ANIMALS.** Dogs and other animals, except seeing-eye dogs, shall not be brought into the Building for other than official purposes.

16. **VEHICULAR AND PEDESTRIAN TRAFFIC.** (a) Drivers of all Vehicles in or about the Building shall drive in a careful and safe manner at all times and shall comply with the signals and directions of Officers and all posted traffic signs; (b) blocking entrances, driveways, walks, loading platforms, or fire hydrants in or about the Building is prohibited; (c) except in emergencies, parking in the Building is not allowed without a permit. Parking without authority, parking in unauthorized locations or in locations reserved for other persons or contrary to the direction of posted signs is prohibited.

17. **WEAPONS AND EXPLOSIVES.** No person while in the Building shall carry firearms, other dangerous or deadly weapons, or explosives, either openly or concealed, except for official purposes.

18. **NONDISCRIMINATION.** There shall be no discrimination by segregation or otherwise against any person or persons because of race, creed, color, or national origin in furnishing, or by refusing to furnish to such person or persons, the use of any facility of a public nature, including all services, privileges, accommodations, and activities provided thereby in the Building.

19. **PENALTIES AND OTHER LAW.** Nothing contained in these rules and regulations shall be construed to abrogate any Federal, State, or local law or regulation or any part thereof, applicable to the City-County Building.

Ronald L. Reinking, P.E., General Manager
Indianapolis-Marion County Building Authority

Indiana Handgun Law, 2005

Appendix   8

Court Notice to ISP of Protective Order

PO-0114   Approved   07-01-02
              Revised   07-01-03

TO: Indiana State Police, Firearms Section

FROM: _____Court _____,

             (_____ Division, Room _____)

DATE: _____

RE: _____ vs.

             _____

             Case Number_____

             Respondent Date of Birth   _____

             Respondent SSN   _____

             Name(s) of Petitioner(s):   _____

             _____

This is to advise you that on the _____ day of _____,
20____, the Court issued an Order for Protection against the above-named
Respondent, _____, prohibiting the use, attempted
use, or threat of physical force and/or finding, *inter alia*, that she/he posed a
credible threat to the safety of _____, the Petitioner,
an intimate partner within the meaning of the federal firearms laws, 18
U.S.C. §922 (g) (8).

The Respondent, _____, states that
she/he does/does not possess a license to carry a handgun.

COPIES TO:

INDIANA STATE POLICE, FIREARMS SECTION, FAX No. (317) 232-0652

RESPONDENT

Appendix   9

Motion and Order to Release Handgun

STATE OF INDIANA   )   IN THE ███████████
)SS:
COUNTY OF MARION   )   CAUSE NO. ██████████

STATE OF INDIANA   )

     VS.   )

██████████████   )

FILED

JAN 1 4 2004

MOTION TO RELEASE HANDGUN

Comes now the Defendant, ██████████ , by counsel, ██████████ and files his

Motion to Release Handgun, and in support thereof, would show the Court, as follows:

    1.   That all charges in the case against ██████████ were dismissed on ██████████

    2.   That ██████████ criminal record has been expunged, due to a misidentification,

all with the agreement and cooperation of the Prosecutor, ██████████

    3.   That ██████████ handgun license has been reinstated by the Indiana State

Police.

    4.   That the ██ Property room or other division of the ██, is maintaining the

handgun, which was confiscated incident to the arrest on misidentification.

    5.   That the serial number of ██████████ handgun is ██████████

    6.   That it is appropriate to release the handgun to ██████████

    WHEREFORE, the Defendant, ██████████ by counsel, ██████████

respectfully prays that the handgun currently in the possession of ██ be released to ██████████

██████████ consistent with ██ policy and procedures, and for all other relief just and proper in the

premises.

Respectfully submitted,

_____

Indiana Handgun Law, 2005

320 North Meridian Street
Suite 311
Indianapolis, Indiana 46204-1719

Certificate of Service

I hereby certify that a copy of the foregoing has been duly served to all parties of record

via United States Mail, first-class, postage prepaid, this the ___14___ day of ███████

██████ County Prosecutor's Office

_____

STATE OF INDIANA) IN THE ██████████████████████████
)SS:
COUNTY OF MARION) CAUSE NO. ████████████████

STATE OF INDIANA)
)
VS.)
)
████████████████)

FILED

ORDER GRANTING MOTION TO RELEASE HANDGUN

Comes now the Court, and after being duly advised in the premises, and grants the

Defendant's Motion to Release Handgun.

IT IS HEREBY ORDERED ADJUDGED AND DECREED, that ████ is ordered to

release to ████████████ the handgun, serial number ████████, currently in the possession of

████, all in accordance with their policies and procedures.

Dated: _1-20-04_

_____
Judge, ████████████████

Distribution:

████████████
320 North Meridian Street
Suite 311
Indianapolis, Indiana 46204-1719

████████████ Prosecutor's Office

167

168

ENDNOTES

1   When handguns are referred to in this text, they are described by various terms including "gun", "weapon", "firearm", "pistol", or "handgun", unless the context and/or specific terms indicate otherwise.

2   The State of Indiana is referred to herein as the "State" or "Indiana".

3   Where Indiana appellate courts are referred to individually, they are referred to as the "Indiana Court of Appeals" or the "Indiana Supreme Court", respectfully. The Indiana Court of Appeals is the intermediate state appellate court. The Indiana Supreme Court is the highest level state appellate court. These two courts are referred to collectively as the "Courts".

4   Throughout this text, the term "license" means an Indiana unlimited license to carry a handgun issued pursuant IC 35-47-2-4(a). However, other terms, such as "Indiana-issued license" or "permit" may be used to refer to an unlimited license, unless the context and/or specific terms indicate otherwise. In strict terms, the handgun permit is properly referred to as "License to Carry Handgun".

5   For the interested reader, I am providing two citations to other works, which I believe represent the best resources in their respective fields. The first text is the definitive federal work: Stephen P. Halbrook, *Firearms Law Deskbook* (2003 ed.). This book is available from Thomson-West at 1-800-328-4880. The second is a state guide covering Florida law: Jon H. Gutmacher, *Florida Firearms Law, Use & Ownership* Book (4th ed.). This book is available from Warlord Publishing at 1-407-650-0770.

6   Any licensee faced with reciprocal carry must be aware of the inherent limits of any given reference text, its biases, and the ability of its author. It is not a defense to a crime that a defendant relied on a given guide.

7   These statistics were determined through a telephone conference with Administrative Assistant, Bruce Bryant, Firearms Section, Indiana State Police, on November 17, 2003, whereby he indicated the current estimate for Indiana handgun licenses was 320,000, with 80% to 85% being unlimited licenses.

8   U.S. Census Bureau data for 2001-2002 at "www.census.gov".

9   Throughout the text, the book is referred to formally as the "Book" or by its complete title, *Indiana Handgun Law*.

10   A comprehensive introduction could begin with the history of development of firearms and their corresponding regulation. This would start with Chinese history beginning with Emperor Wu Di from 156-87 B.C.. While not inventing gunpowder, it is believed that his chemists began to experiment with similar compounds for medicinal purposes. Ultimately, this led to the creation of gunpowder a few centuries later, although the exact time is unclear. Such history should not be disregarded by anyone wanting a comprehensive understanding of present-day gun law, as current law is substantially shaped by its historical underpinnings.

11   The United States of America is referred to in this Book as the "United States" or "Nation".

12   *See generally Trotter v. Nelson*, 684 N.E.2d 1150, 1152 (Ind.1997) (in determining public policy, the courts look to the constitution and to the statutory law of the state); *see also Allstate Insurance Company v. Boles*, 481 N.E.2d 1096, 1099 (Ind. 1985) (if policy supporting legal doctrine is outdated, the law may be changed based on public policy at the present time).

13   *See, e.g.,* Homeland Security Act of 2002.

14   The United States Congress is referred to as the "U.S. Congress" or "Congress". The laws of the Congress are codified in the United States Code, which will be referred to as "USC".

15   *See* 6 U.S.C. § 1, *et seq.* (codification of Homeland Security Act of 2002). An excellent compilation of relevant federal law enacted post-September 11, 2001, is entitled *Guide to Homeland Security* (2003 ed.), and is available from Thomson-West at 1-800-328-4880.

16   18 U.S.C. § 1993 (criminal statutory scheme for acts of terrorism against mass transportation terminals and vehicles).

17   *See generally* John E. Nowak and Ronald D. Rotunda, *Constitutional Law* § 1.1 (4th ed. 1991) (the power of the U.S. Supreme Court to determine the constitutionality and, therefore, the validity of the other branches of government has been firmly established as a basic component of the American system of government).

18   The 2nd Amendment to the United States Constitution, which is included in the first ten amendments, collectively known as the Bill of Rights, was ratified effective December 15, 1791, which provides: "A well regulated Militia, being necessary to the security of a free state, the right of the people to keep and bear arms, shall not be infringed."

19   The United States Constitution is referred to in this Book as the "U.S. Constitution" or "Constitution".

20   Article I § 32 of the Indiana Constitution provides: "The people shall have a right to bear arms, for the defense of themselves and the state."

21   Under our system of government, it is quite possible that multiple state and federal laws, rules, and regulations, criminal or civil, may encompass a single issue. Thus, there may be overlap of crimes, allowing a violator to be tried at a state or federal level. This is a very technical area, and raises double jeopardy and other issues, which are beyond the scope of this Book.

22   *See, e.g., Stratton v. State,* 791 N.E.2d 220, 224 (Ind.Ct.App. 2003) (judiciary is to enforce legislative intent, but when a statute is ambiguous, judicial interpretation is necessary). The Indiana Legislature, moreover, has enacted a statutory scheme at IC 1-1-4-1 to assist with construction of its statutes, which provides: "The construction of all statutes of this state shall be by the following rules, unless the construction is plainly repugnant to the intent of the legislature or of the context of the statute: (1) Words and phrases shall be taken in their plain, or ordinary and usual, sense. Technical words and phrases having a peculiar and appropriate meaning in law shall be understood according to their technical import. (2) Words importing joint authority to three (3) or more persons shall be construed as authority to a majority of the persons, unless otherwise declared in the statute giving authority. (3) Words importing the singular number only may be also applied to the plural of persons and things. (4) Words importing the masculine gender only may be extended to females also. (5)When a statute requires

an act to be done which, by law, an agent or deputy as well may do as the principal, the requisition is satisfied by the performance of the act by an authorized agent or deputy. (6) When a person is required to be disinterested or indifferent in acting on any question or matter affecting other parties, consanguinity or affinity within the sixth degree, inclusive, by the civil law rules, or within the degree of second cousin, inclusive, disqualifies the person from acting, except by consent of the parties."

23 The Indiana General Assembly is referred to in this Book as the "Legislature" or "General Assembly". All statutory law enacted by the Legislature is codified in the Indiana Code ("IC"). Moreover, Indiana's statutory law found in the Indiana Code is very logically organized, and may be easily remembered by a simple phrase "TACS": Title, Article, Chapter, and Section, respectively. The title is the statutory book number by topical area. For instance, Title 35 is the criminal code. The subset of a title is an article sub-topic. Article 47 of the criminal code covers weapons and instruments of violence. Articles have chapters. Article 47, for instance, has 11 chapters. Sections are specific provisions of chapters.

24 Criminal defenses are of two types. The first type of defense is a general defense, whereby the defense shows that the prosecution did not establish an element of the crime, which is always the prosecution's burden. The second type of defense is an affirmative criminal defense, which allows a person to do something that would ordinarily be criminal, such as use deadly force, in certain circumstances. All elements of the crime are met, but it is excused.

25 IC 35-41-3-2(d) (force, including deadly force, may be used in circumstances to protect a pirated airliner over Indiana airspace).

26 *See generally Healthscript v. State*, 740 N.E.2d 562, 563-64 (Ind. Ct. App. 2000) (the Legislature can delegate to an administrative agency some role in criminal matters, without violating separation of powers).

27 The administrative bodies created and empowered by the Legislature enact rules and regulations that are compiled in the Indiana Administrative Code ("IAC"). The administrative rules of the administrative agencies of Congress are compiled in the Code of Federal Regulations ("CFR").

28   *See generally Evansville State Hospital v. Perry*, 549 N.E.2d 44, 46 (Ind.Ct.App. 1989) (administrative boards, agencies, and officers have no common law or inherent powers, but only such authority as is conferred upon them by statutory enactment).

29   68 IAC 1-7-1(b) (weapons prohibited on riverboat casinos).

30   39 CFR 232.1(l) (no person while on postal property may carry firearms openly or concealed).

31   *See generally Lloyd Corp. v. Tanner*, 407 U.S. 551 (1972) (even public property does not lose its private character merely because the public generally is invited to use it for designated purposes); *see also Stout v. State*, 479 N.E.2d 563, 566-67 (Ind. 1985) (private landowner has control over premises). In fact, the author has recently reviewed several leases that have clauses with rules and regulations regarding firearms. One lease was for a commercial business, wherein the proposed terms of the lessee's lease, precluded the potential lessee from having firearms on the premises. The second was an apartment lease that precluded possession of firearms by the lessee in the leased apartment. While not a criminal act, such breach by the lessee, would constitute a breach of contract (lease) subject to remedies, up to, and including, eviction.

32   *See Newson v. State*, 785 N.E.2d 1155, 1158 (Ind.Ct.App. 2003) (leaving a handgun in passenger's seat at a school loading dock, while dropping off person, even with a valid handgun license, is a felony).

33   Article I § 32 of the Indiana Constitution.

34   The Legislature has specifically acknowledged that its statutory law is subject to the Indiana Constitution by IC 1-1-2-1, which provides: "The law governing this state is declared to be: First. The Constitution of the United States and of this state. Second. All statutes of the general assembly of the state in force, and not inconsistent with such constitutions. Third. All statutes of the United States in force, and relating to subjects over which congress has power to legislate for the states, and not inconsistent with the Constitution of the United States. Fourth. The common law of England . . . ."

35   *See, e.g., Dozier v. State,* 709 N.E.2d 27, 31 (Ind.Ct.App. 1999). Selected text from the *Dozier* opinion is as follows: "The constitutional right to bear arms is not absolute. Our Supreme Court has determined that '[t]he Legislature has the power, in the interest of public safety and welfare, to provide reasonable regulations for the use of firearms which may be readily concealed, such as pistols.' *Matthews v. State,* 237 Ind. 677, 686, 148 N.E.2d 334, 338 (1958) (rejecting an Article I § 32 challenge to handgun legislation). The statutes at issue in this case require a person to have a license to carry a handgun, increase the class of the offense for carrying a handgun on school property, and prohibit the possession of a handgun by a person under eighteen years of age. These statutes are in the interest of public safety and provide reasonable regulation for the use of handguns. Dozier's constitutional challenge thus fails. Judgment affirmed."

36   *Id.*

37   The statute that prohibits carrying a handgun without a license and making it a criminal act is IC 35-47-2-1, which provides: "(a) Except as provided in subsection (b) and section 2 of this chapter, a person shall not carry a handgun in any vehicle or on or about the person's body, except in the person's dwelling, on the person's property or fixed place of business, without a license issued under this chapter being in the person's possession. (b) Unless the person's right to possess a firearm has been restored under IC 3-7-13-5 or IC 33-4-5-7, a person who has been convicted of domestic battery under IC 35-42-2-1.3 may not possess or carry a handgun in any vehicle or on or about the person's body in the person's dwelling or on the person's property or fixed place of business."

38   *Id.*

39   *Id.*

40   The statutory exceptions to the requirement of the   licensing statute are logical, and are codified at IC 35-47-2-2, and provide: "Section 1 of this chapter [requiring licensing] does not apply to: (1) marshals; (2) sheriffs; (3) the commissioner of the department of correction or persons authorized by him in writing to carry firearms; (4) judicial officers; (5) law enforcement officers; (6) members of the armed forces of the United States or of the national guard or organized reserves while they are on duty; (7) regularly enrolled members of any organization duly

authorized to purchase or receive such weapons from the United States or from this state who are at or are going to or from their place of assembly or target practice; (8) employees of the United States duly authorized to carry handguns; (9) employees of express companies when engaged in company business; (10) any person engaged in the business of manufacturing, repairing, or dealing in firearms or the agent or representative of any such person having in his possession, using, or carrying a handgun in the usual or ordinary course of that business; or (11) any person while carrying a handgun unloaded and in a secure wrapper from the place of purchase to his dwelling or fixed place of business, or to a place of repair or back to his dwelling or fixed place of business, or in moving from one dwelling or business to another."

41   The statute delineating the two types of handgun permits, qualified and unlimited, is IC 35-47-2-4, and provides: "(a) Licenses to carry handguns shall be either qualified or unlimited. A qualified license shall be issued for hunting and target practice. The superintendent may adopt rules imposing limitations on the use and carrying of handguns under a license when handguns are carried by a licensee as a condition of employment. Unlimited licenses shall be issued for the purpose of the protection of life and property. (b) In addition to the application fee, the fee for a qualified license shall be five dollars ($5), and the fee for an unlimited license shall be fifteen dollars ($15). The superintendent shall charge a five dollar ($5) fee for the issuance of a duplicate license to replace a lost or damaged license. These fees shall be deposited by the superintendent with the treasurer of the state. (c) Licensed dealers are exempt from the payment of fees specified in subsection (b) for a qualified license or an unlimited license. (d) The following officers of this state or the United States who have been honorably retired by a lawfully created pension board or its equivalent after at least twenty (20) years of service or because of a disability are exempt from the payment of fees specified in subsection (b): (1) Police officers. (2) Sheriffs or their deputies. (3) Law enforcement officers. (4) Correctional officers."

42   The location to make application, and the content of the application itself, are specified by statute, IC 35-47-2-3, which provides: "(a) A person desiring a license to carry a handgun shall apply: (1) to the chief of police or corresponding law enforcement officer of the municipality in which the applicant resides; (2) if that municipality has no such officer, or if the applicant does not reside in a municipality, to the sheriff of the county in which the applicant resides after the applicant has obtained an application form prescribed by the Superintendent; or (3) if the applicant is a resident of another state and has a regular place of business or

175

employment in Indiana, to the sheriff of the county in which the applicant has a regular place of business or employment. (b)   The law enforcement agency which accepts an application for a handgun license shall collect a ten dollar ($10) application fee, five dollars ($5) of which shall be refunded if the license is not issued. Except as provided in subsection (h), the fee shall be: (1) deposited into the law enforcement agency's firearms training fund or other appropriate training activities fund; and (2) used by the agency for purposes of: (A) training law enforcement officers in the proper use of firearms or other law enforcement duties; or (B) purchasing for the law enforcement officers employed by the law enforcement agency firearms, or firearm related equipment, or both. The state board of accounts shall establish rules for the proper accounting and expenditure of funds collected under this subsection. (c) The officer to whom the application is made shall ascertain the applicant's name, full address, length of residence in the community, whether the applicant's residence is located within the limits of any city or town, the applicant's occupation, place of business or employment, criminal record, if any, and convictions (minor traffic offenses excepted), age, race, sex, nationality, date of birth, citizenship, height, weight, build, color of hair, color of eyes, scars and marks, whether the applicant has previously held an Indiana license to carry a handgun and, if so, the serial number of the license and year issued, whether the applicant's license has ever been suspended or revoked, and if so, the year and reason for the suspension or revocation, and the applicant's reason for desiring a license.   The officer to whom the application is made shall conduct an investigation into the applicant's official records and verify thereby the applicant's character and reputation, and shall in addition verify for accuracy the information contained in the application, and shall forward this information together with his recommendation for approval or disapproval and one (1) set of legible and classifiable fingerprints of the applicant to the superintendent. (d) The superintendent may make whatever further investigation the superintendent deems necessary. Whenever disapproval is recommended, the officer to whom the application is made shall provide the superintendent and the applicant with the officer's complete and specific reasons, in writing, for the recommendation of disapproval. (e)   If it appears to the superintendent that the applicant has a proper reason for carrying a handgun and is of good character and reputation and a proper person to be so licensed, the superintendent shall issue to the applicant a qualified or an unlimited license to carry any handgun lawfully possessed by the applicant. The original license shall be delivered to the licensee. A copy shall be delivered to the officer to whom the application for license was made. A copy shall be retained by the superintendent for at least four (4) years. This license shall be valid for a period of four (4) years from the date of issue. The license of police officers, sheriffs or their deputies, and law enforcement officers of the United States government who have been honorably retired by a lawfully created pension board or its equivalent after twenty (20) or more years of service, shall be valid for the life of such individuals. However, such lifetime licenses are automatically revoked if the license holder does not remain a proper person. (f) At the time a license is issued and delivered to a licensee under subsection (e), the superintendent shall include with the license information concerning handgun safety rules that: (1) neither opposes nor supports an individual's right to bear arms; and (2) is: (A) recommended by a nonprofit educational organization that is dedicated to providing education on safe handling and use of firearms; (B) prepared by the state police department; and (C) approved by the superintendent. The superintendent may not deny a license under this section because the information required under this subsection is unavailable at the time the superintendent would otherwise issue a license. The state police department may accept private donations or grants to defray the cost of printing and mailing the information required under this subsection. (g) A license to carry a handgun shall not be issued to any person who: (1) has been convicted of a felony; (2) is under eighteen (18) years of age; (3) is under twenty-three (23) years of age if the person has been adjudicated a delinquent child for an act that would be a felony if committed by an adult; or (4) has been arrested for a Class A or Class B felony, or any other felony that was committed while armed with a deadly weapon or that involved the use of violence, if a court has found probable cause to believe that the person committed the offense charged. In the case of an arrest under subdivision (4), a license to carry a handgun may be issued to a person who has been acquitted of the specific offense charged or if the charges for the specific offense are dismissed. The superintendent shall prescribe all forms to be used in connection with the administration of this chapter. (h) If the law enforcement agency that charges a fee under subsection (b) is a city or town law enforcement agency, the fee shall be deposited in the law enforcement continuing education fund established under IC 5-2-8-2. (i) If a person who holds a valid license to carry a handgun issued under this chapter: (1) changes the person's name; or (2) changes the person's address; the person shall, not later than sixty (60) days after the date of the change, notify the superintendent, in writing, of the person's new name or new address. (j) The state police shall indicate on the form for a license to carry a handgun the notification requirements of subsection (i)."

177

43   The statute allowing for suspension or revocation of a license is IC 35-47-2-5, and provides: "(a)   The superintendent may suspend or revoke any license issued under this chapter if he has reasonable grounds to believe that the person's license should be suspended or revoked. (b) Documented evidence that a person is not a 'proper person' to be licensed as defined by IC 35-47-1-7, or is prohibited under section (3)(g)(4) of this chapter from being issued a license, shall be grounds for immediate suspension or revocation of a license previously issued under this chapter. However, if a license is suspended or revoked based solely on an arrest under section (3)(g)(4) of this chapter, the license shall be reinstated upon the acquittal of the defendant in that case or upon the dismissal of the charges for the specific offense.(c) A person who fails to promptly return his license after written notice of suspension or revocation commits a Class A misdemeanor. The observation of a handgun license in the possession of a person whose license has been suspended or revoked constitutes a sufficient basis for the arrest of that person for violation of this subsection. (d) The superintendent shall establish rules under IC 4-22-2 concerning the procedure for suspending or revoking a person's license."

44   The statute that acknowledges and grants reciprocity to foreign handgun permits is IC 35-47-2-21, and provides: "(a) Retail dealers' licenses issued by other states or foreign countries will not be recognized in Indiana except for sales at wholesale. (b) Licenses to carry handguns, issued by other states or foreign countries, will be recognized according to the terms thereof but only while the holders are not residents of Indiana."

45   IC 35-47-2-1(a) (handgun carry prohibition statute).

46   The "carrying" of a handgun without a license can be through actual carrying or constructive possession as analyzed herein.

47   IC 35-47-2-1(a) (license required to carry handgun outside dwelling and property or fixed place of business).

48   Not all such rights have been recognized as fundamental. This is a very complex area of constitutional law, and is beyond the scope of this Book. The interested reader is urged to review the cited constitutional law treatise by Nowak & Rotunda.

49   Indiana's criminal statutory provisions are published in Title 35 of the IC, which is referred to as the "criminal code" or "penal code", unless the context indicates otherwise.

50   IC 35-47-2-1(a) (license required to carry handgun outside dwelling and property or fixed place of business).

51   This statute has been re-codified and was formerly IC 35-23-4-3, although caselaw under that statute is generally applicable to the re-codification.

52   IC 35-47-2-1(b) (person convicted of domestic battery may not carry or possess a firearm); *see also* IC 35-47-4-6 (person who has been convicted of domestic battery who knowingly or intentionally possesses a firearm commits a Class A misdemeanor).

53   The statute defining who is a serious violent felon is IC 35-47-4-5, which provides: "(a) As used in this section, 'serious violent felon' means a person who has been convicted of: (1) committing a serious violent felony in: (A) Indiana; or (B) any other jurisdiction in which the elements of the crime for which the conviction was entered are substantially similar to the elements of a serious violent felony; or (2) attempting to commit or conspiring to commit a serious violent felony in: (A) Indiana as provided under IC 35-41-5-1 or IC 35-41-5-2; or (B) any other jurisdiction in which the elements of the crime for which the conviction was entered are substantially similar to the elements of attempting to commit or conspiring to commit a serious violent felony. (b) As used in this section, 'serious violent felony' means: (1) murder; (2) voluntary manslaughter; (3) reckless homicide not committed by means of a vehicle; (4) battery as a: (A) Class A felony; (B) Class B felony; (C) Class C felony; (5) aggravated battery; (6) kidnaping; (7) criminal confinement; (8) rape; (9) criminal deviate conduct; (10) child molesting; (11) sexual battery as a Class C felony; (12) robbery; (13) carjacking; (14) arson as a Class A felony or Class B felony; (15) burglary as a Class A felony or Class B felony; (16) assisting a criminal as a Class C felony; (17) resisting law enforcement as a Class B felony or Class C felony; (18) escape as a Class B felony or Class C felony; (19) trafficking with an inmate as a Class C felony; (20) criminal gang intimidation; (21) stalking as a Class B felony or Class C felony; (22) incest; (23) dealing in or manufacturing cocaine, a narcotic drug, or methamphetamine; (24) dealing in a schedule I, II, or III controlled substance; (25) dealing in a schedule IV controlled substance; or (26) dealing in a schedule V controlled substance. (c) A

serious violent felon who knowingly or intentionally possesses a firearm commits unlawful possession of a firearm by a serious violent felon, a Class B felony."

54   There are a host of other criminal and/or civil preclusions to carry/ possession of a handgun, both state and federal. For instance, it is a standard term of probation for most all crimes that the probationer not be allowed to possess firearms.

55   IC 35-47-2-1(b) (person convicted of domestic battery may not carry or possess a firearm).

56   There are attorney general opinions that further explain, at least according to the Indiana Attorney General, what law enforcement officers fall within these exceptions, such as non-salaried game wardens who are excepted from licensing. 1938 Op.Atty.Gen. 105. However, attorney general opinions do not have the force of law in Indiana. *See generally Medical Licensing Board of Indiana v. Ward, D.C.,* 449 N.E.2d 1129, 1138 (Ind.Ct.App. 1983) (basic tenet of Indiana law that appellate courts are not bound by official opinions of the attorney general).

57   *See State v. Turner,* 567 N.E.2d 783, 784 (Ind. 1991) (an ambiguity as to whether a common carrier was an express company under the handgun licensing statute required dismissal of the charge against the driver for the common carrier).

58   IC 35-47-2-1(a) (handgun carry prohibition statute).

59   IC 35-47-2-1(a) (license required to carry handgun outside dwelling and property or fixed place of business).

60   IC 35-47-2-2 (persons exempted from licensing to carry or possess handgun).

61   The statutory crimes for handgun regulation violations are codified in IC 35-47-2-23, which provides: "(a) A person who violates section 3, 4, 5, 14, 15, or 16 of this chapter commits a Class B misdemeanor. (b) A person who violates section 7, 17, or 18 of this chapter commits a Class C felony. (c) A person who violates section 1 of this chapter commits a Class A misdemeanor. However, the offense is a Class C felony: (1) if the offense is committed: (A) on

or in school property; (B) within one thousand (1,000) feet of school property; or (C) on a school bus; or (2) if the person: (A) has a prior conviction of any offense under: (i) this subsection; or (ii) subsection (d); or (B) has been convicted of a felony within fifteen (15) years before the date of the offense. (d) A person who violates section 22 of this chapter commits a Class A misdemeanor. However, the offense is a Class D felony if the person has a prior conviction of any offense under this subsection or subsection (c), or if the person has been convicted of a felony within fifteen (15) years before the date of the offense."

62   *See, e.g., Wallace v. State,* 722 N.E.2d 910, 913 (Ind.Ct.App. 2000) (to convict a defendant of carrying a handgun without a license, the prosecution must prove that the defendant (1) carried a handgun, (2) in a vehicle or on or about his person, (3) in a place other than his dwelling, property, or fixed place of business).

63   *See, e.g., Harris v. State,* 716 N.E.2d 406, 411 (Ind. 1999) (once the prosecution establishes the defendant carried a handgun, on or about his person, and away from dwelling or business, the burden shifts to defendant).

64   *Id.*

65   *Id.*

66   *See, e.g., Beck v. State,* 414 N.E.2d 970, 973 (Ind.Ct.App. 1981) (in order for defendant to meet secure wrapper exception to licensing scheme, he must prove that the gun was unloaded and in a secure wrapper).

67   *See, e.g., Seel v. State,* 739 N.E.2d 170, 172 (Ind.Ct.App. 2000) (guns in storage unit, when defendant arrested at a different place, not being carried).

68   *See Ward v.State,* 438 N.E.2d 750, 753 (Ind. 1982) (it is important to note that there is a difference between affirmative defenses, as some may actually negate an element of the crime; it is unconstitutional to place the burden of persuasion on the defendant, when proving the defense becomes tantamount to requiring the defendant to negate an element of the crime).

69   IC 35-47-2-23 (classes of crimes for violation of the handgun regulation statutes).

70   The sentence for a Class A misdemeanor is codified at IC 35-50-3-2, and provides: "A person who commits a Class A misdemeanor shall be imprisoned for a fixed term of not more than one (1) year; in addition, he may be fined not more than five thousand dollars ($5,000)."

71   IC 35-47-2-23(c)(1) (Class C felony if the offense is committed on or in school property, within 1,000 feet of school property, or on a school bus).

72   *See generally Henderson v. State*, 715 N.E.2d 833, 835 (Ind. 1999) (the "on" a person occurs when a person has direct physical control over the handgun; the "about" occurs when a person has the intent and capability to maintain dominion and control presently over the gun).

73   *See Wallace*, 722 N.E.2d at 913 (carrying of handgun can be shown by actual carry or constructive possession).

74   *See generally Nichols v. State*, 638 N.E.2d 1358 (Ind.Ct.App. 1997).

75   *See generally Woods v. State*, 471 N.E.2d 691, 694 (Ind. 1984) (where defendant had loaned his vehicle to another person, but the vehicle had been returned for four days and he had dominion and control of the vehicle, it was sufficient to sustain the conviction for carrying without a license).

76   *See, e.g., State v. Hill*, 688 N.E.2d 1280, 1283 (Ind.Ct.App. 1997) (constructive possession may be inferred when circumstantial evidence points to the defendant's knowledge of the presence of the handgun, even if his control is not exclusive).

77   *See generally Parson v. State*, 431 N.E.2d 870, 873 (Ind.Ct.App. 1982) (exclusive and non-exclusive dominion over handgun for carrying without a license can support conviction); *see also Haynes v. State*, 431 N.E.2d 83, 87 (Ind. 1982).

78   *See, e.g., Ferrell v. State*, 656 N.E.2d 839, 842 (Ind.Ct.App. 1995) (constructive possession of a handgun may be inferred from the facts if there is circumstantial evidence to point to the defendant's knowledge of the handgun).

79   *See generally Wallace,* 722 N.E.2d at 913 (conviction for carrying without a license can be sustained on actual carry or constructive possession).

80   *See Seel,* 739 N.E.2d at 172-73 (where defendant arrested at a location different from his storage unit with stored guns, no evidence to sustain conviction of carrying or constructive possession of a handgun without a license).

81   *See generally* IC 35-47-1-1 through 35-47-1-13 (definitions of terms for Article 47 on weapons, wherein term "dwelling" is not defined).

82   The statute defining a "dwelling" in the penal code is IC 35-41-1-10, which provides: "'Dwelling' means a building, structure, or other enclosed space, permanent or temporary, movable or fixed, that is a person's home or place of lodging."

83   The statute that indicates that this definition of dwelling applies throughout the criminal statutes is IC 35-41-1-3, which provides: "The definitions in this chapter [which include 'dwelling'] apply throughout this title and to all other statutes relating to penal offenses."

84   *See Robertson v. State,* 765 N.E.2d 138, 139-140 (Ind. 2002) (interpreting the legislative intent of the statute to not apply to areas outside of a person's apartment, vacating the Court of Appeals opinion, which held that "the area immediately outside of a person's apartment is a part of that person's dwelling", and affirming the conviction of the trial court; but it is important to note that Justice Rucker dissented, and advocated for the Court of Appeals position.)

85   IC 35-41-1-10 (definition of dwelling).

86   *See Robertson,* 765 N.E.2d at 140 (area outside apartment not dwelling).

87   *See Winters v. State,* 719 N.E.2d 1279, 1282 (Ind.Ct.App. 1999) (motel room where defendant was found was not dwelling, where no evidence defendant registered, paid for, or intended to sleep there).

88   *See Jones v. State,* 536 N.E.2d 490, 492 (Ind. 1989) (defendant did not reside at

mother's home, although she had before, at the time she used firearm there to attempt to kill her mother and father, and as such, this was not her dwelling).

89   *See generally Winters*, 719 N.E.2d at 1282 (presence in motel room standing alone, does not make same temporary dwelling).

90   *See, e.g., Seel,* 739 N.E.2d at 173 (undisputed fact that the weapons were found in Seel's rented storage facility is, as a matter of law, insufficient to support the inference that the defendant at one time carried or will carry the weapons on his person or in a vehicle).

91   *See generally* IC 35-47-1-1 through 35-47-1-13 (definitions of terms for Article 47 on weapons, wherein "property" is not defined).

92   The penal code's definition of the term "property" is codified at IC 35-41-1-23, and provides: "(a) 'Property' means anything of value. The term includes: (1) a gain or advantage or anything that might reasonably be regarded as such by the beneficiary; (2) real property, personal property, money, labor, and services; (3) intangibles; (4) commercial instruments; (5) written instruments concerning labor, services, or property; (6) written instruments otherwise of value to the owner, such as a public record, deed, will, credit card, or letter of credit; (7) a signature to a written instrument; (8) extension of credit; (9) trade secrets; (10) contract rights, choses-in-action, and other interests in or claims to wealth; (11) electricity, gas, oil, and water; (12) captured or domestic animals, birds, and fish; (13) food and drink; and (14) human remains. (b) Property is that 'of another person' if the other person has a possessory or proprietary interest in it, even if an accused person also has an interest in that property."

93   It is clear from the *Robertson* case, *supra,* and innumerable cases on point, that the Indiana Courts look at legislative intent to foster an application of a statute in a fair, consistent, and predictable manner. To apply the penal code's property definition would not only frustrate the intent of this statute, which is obviously intended to be limited to real property, but also directly conflict with the prohibition of allowing a person to possess a handgun in a motor vehicle without a license.

94   To be consistent with property law, and the clear legislative intent in the penal code's criminal provisions regarding carry, a real property interest will not extend to a property licenses (not to be confused with a handgun license) to do and conduct actions on real property. *See generally Industrial Disposal Corporation of America v. City of East Chicago, Department of Water Works,* 407 N.E.2d 1203, 1205 (Ind.Ct.App. 1980); 28 C.J.S.

Easements § 2. For example, a ticket to a movie theater would be a license, not a grant of a property interest, and not allow carry thereat without a handgun license. This is a technical area of law beyond the scope of this Book.

95   *See Winters*, 719 N.E.2d at 1279 (hotel room may not be temporary dwelling).

96   *See generally Dunbar v. State*, 319 N.E.2d 630, 632 (Ind.Ct.App. 1974) (public alley behind residence is not part of abode).

97   *See generally Estate of Heck v. Stoffer*, 786 N.E.2d 265, 268-70 (Ind. 2003) (gun owner's duty of care).

98   *See* IC 35-47-2-1(a) (handgun licensing exceptions do not apply to dwellings that may be mobile).

99   IC 35-47-2-2 (transportation unloaded and in a secure wrapper).

100   *See, e.g., Gray v. State*, 305 N.E.2d 886, 888 (Ind.Ct.App. 1974) (secure wrapper must be such as to prevent immediate or ready access to the injurious capabilities of weapons thus carried).

101   *See Beck*, 414 N.E.2d at 972-973 (because defendant produced the gun from under the seat and the cylinder from a grocery bag in the backseat, the jury could have easily inferred that defendant just disassembled the gun and placed the cylinder in the bag, and verdict was supported by the evidence).

102   Field stripped is a condition referred to for proper cleaning of the weapon. It does not include disassembly of the weapon as would be done by a factory-certified armorer, such as part by part, as this would be a dangerous proposition. This is because the lay owner would have to disassemble a complex weapon, a task not within his/her scope of experience and training.

103   IC 35-47-2-1(a) (license required to carry a handgun outside dwelling and property or fixed place of business).

104   *See* Chapter 1 (carry without a license generally prohibited).

105   *See Dozier*, 709 N.E.2d at 31 (Supreme Court has held that Legislature has power, in interest of public safety, to provide reasonable regulations on handguns).

106   *See generally* IC 35-47-2-3 (handgun application statute and directions to Superintendent thereunder).

107   IC 35-47-2-3(2) (handgun application statute, whereby it directs the Superintendent to establish application form).

108   IC 35-47-2-3(e) (Superintendent shall issue if proper person and reason).

109   IC 35-47-2-3 (handgun application statute).

110   IC 35-47-2-3(e) (license valid for four years).

111   The statute on renewal and the time for accepting an initial or renewal application is IC 35-47-2-6, which provides: "Every initial application for any license under this chapter shall be granted or rejected within sixty (60) days after the application is filed. If the application for renewal of an existing license is filed within thirty (30) days of its expiration, the existing license is automatically extended until the application for renewal is passed upon."

112   IC 35-47-2-4(b) ($5.00 fee for duplicate license).

113   IC 35-47-2-3(i) (name and address change notification requirement for licensees).

114   IC 35-47-2-5 (suspension and revocation statute).

115   The statute allowing for removal of a disability precluding licensing is IC 35-47-2-20, and provides: "(a) A full pardon from the governor of Indiana for: (1) a felony other than a felony that is included in IC 35-42; or a violation of this chapter; removes

any disability under this chapter imposed because of that offense, if fifteen (15) years have elapsed between the time of the offense and the application for a license under this chapter. (b) A conditional pardon described in IC 11-9-2-4 for: (1) felony; or (2) a violation of this chapter; removes a disability under this chapter if the superintendent determines after an investigation that circumstances have changed since the pardoned conviction was entered to such an extent that the pardoned person is likely to handle handguns in compliance with the law."

116   IC 35-47-2-4(a) (types of handgun licenses).

117   *See* phone interview with Indiana State Police, Administrative Assistant, Firearms Section, on November 17, 2003.

118   IC 35-47-2-4(a) (qualified license shall be for hunting and target practice).

119   IC 35-47-2-4(b) (qualified and unlimited license statute addressing processing and license fees).

120   IC 35-47-2-4(a) (unlimited license for purpose of protection of life and property).

121   IC 35-47-2-3 (a) (apply for handgun license through chief of police of municipality, or if none, the county sheriff).

122   *Id.*

123   In Marion County, for instance, a resident desiring a handgun license application, goes to the citizens' services office on the 1st floor of the City-County Building, East Wing. With the application, there is a detailed information sheet provided.

124   *See* IC 35-47-2-3(a)(2) (county sheriff if not living in municipality or no such officer of municipality).

125   The application is titled "Application for Handgun License" and is

Indiana form 36991.

126   *See* IC 35-47-2-3 (compare against and with the questions of the application).

127   *See generally* IC 35-47-2-3 (required data that would have to be obtained in a legible form for Superintendent to issue license). Additionally, in Marion County, for example, the law enforcement agency requires the application to be typed. IPD Form 3-4-50 R9.

128   This warning is based on a "proper person" being one who does not make a false statement of material fact on his/her application. *See* IC 35-47-1-7 (proper person definition). *See also* IC 35-47-2-23 (violation of other statutory provisions make a material false statement of fact subject to conviction for a Class C felony).

129   *See also* IC 35-47-2-17 (prohibiting providing false information on license application).

130   *See Indiana Notary Public Pamphlet* SP 6 (R6/10-97), Sue Anne Gilroy, Secretary of State, page 5.

131   IC 35-47-2-3(b) ($5.00 shall be refunded if license not issued).

132   In Marion County, for instance, under IPD Form 3-4-50 R9, the application fee is to be paid in cash.

133   This is stated on the face of the application.

134   IC 35-47-2-4(b) ($5.00 license fee for qualified license and $15.00 license fee for unlimited license).

135   *See* IC 35-47-2-3(c) (information for application for handgun license to be obtained by officer to whom application is made).

136   The minor traffic offenses not excepted are enumerated in administrative

rule, 240 IAC 3-4-1, which provides: "(1) An applicant need not list traffic arrests or traffic convictions on his application except: (A) Driving Under the Influence of Alcohol, Drugs or Narcotics; (B) Reckless Driving; (C) Fleeing a Police Officer; and (D) Any charges related to injury or death."

137   *See* IC 35-47-2-3(c) (information for application for handgun license to be obtained by officer to whom application is made).

138   *Id.*

139   *Id.*

140   The three criminal data bases available to local and/or state law enforcement officers for records inquiries are IDACS, NCIC, and NLETS. IDACS is the Indiana-based system and is formally known as the Indiana Data and Communications System. The Indiana State Police's website, at "www.in.gov/isp/idacs", describes these systems as follows: "The Indiana Data Communications System (IDACS) is a computerized law enforcement/criminal justice communications and information storage and retrieval system.   This system is designed to serve as a tool in providing more effective and efficient law enforcement for both the citizens of this State and, through interfacing with the National Crime Information Center (NCIC) computer, and the National Law Enforcement Telecommunications System (NLETS) computer, the Nation as a whole."

141   IC 35-47-2-3(c).

142   *Id.*

143   IC 35-47-2-6 (application shall be granted or rejected within sixty days).

144   IC 35-47-2-3(d) (when disapproval is recommended, the officer to whom application is made shall provide the Superintendent and the applicant with the officer's complete and specific reasons, in writing, of the recommendation for disapproval).

145   *See generally* IC 35-47-2-3(e) (if it appears to the Superintendent that applicant is "proper person" and has "proper reason", the license shall be issued).

146   IC 35-47-1-7 (proper person definition and information).

147   IC 35-47-2-3(g) (a license to carry a handgun shall not be issued to any person who has certain additional matters in background).

148   The administrative rule is 240 IAC 3-1-1, which provides: "(1) The Superintendent of the Indiana State Police Department will not issue a firearm license which would place a licensee in contradiction of Federal Firearm Law. (2) A person is an improper person if: (A) He has a history of minor criminal activity which would give rise to a reasonable belief that the applicant has a propensity for violent or emotionally unstable conduct. (B) He is found, upon a standard of reasonable belief, not to be emotionally stable. . . .(D) He makes a false statement of material fact on his application. (3) A person will have a sufficient reason for the issuance of an unlimited firearm license if he states a legal purpose for desiring such license. (4) On the statement of a reason for meeting the criteria [of the foregoing #3] the burden of denying a license due to improper or insufficient reason shall be upon the Superintendent. (5) The Superintendent may issue a restricted license when the license is issued for a person's employment."

149   A "proper reason" is defined by statute, IC 35-47-1-9, which provides: "'Proper reason' means for the defense of oneself or the State of Indiana." This definition is in apparent conflict with the breath of the statute authorizing types of licenses. *See* IC 35-47-2-4(a). However, this issue is mooted by the administrative rule making a proper reason any legal reason. *See* 240 IAC 3-1-1 (sufficient reason for issuance of license if a legal purpose).

150   IC 35-47-2-3(e) (license issued shall be valid for a period of four years from date of issue).

151   IC 35-47-2-6 (if application for renewal of existing license is filed within thirty days of expiration, the license is automatically extended until renewal is passed upon).

152   IC 35-47-2-4(b) ($5.00 fee for duplicate license).

153   *See* P.L.27-2001, SEC.1; P.L.12–2001, SEC.1.

154   IC 35-47-2-3(i) (notification of Superintendent of name or address change within sixty days).

155   *See generally* IC 35-47-2-3(i) (implications if notification by the Superintendent was sent to the wrong address or person, including criminal implications if the license holder was deemed to have notice, and this may be a misdemeanor).

156   *See* IC 35-47-2-5(a) (Superintendent may suspend or revoke license if he has reasonable grounds).

157   The administrative rule regarding suspension on written request of local law enforcement is 240 IAC 3-2-1, which provides: "(1) The Superintendent will temporarily suspend a firearm license upon the written request of a local police department, sheriff's department, prosecutor or full time police officer, without prior hearing. (2) The request for suspension must state reasonable grounds for such suspension. (3) Upon suspension, the licensee will be given notice of right to an immediate hearing and grounds for the suspension. (4) An authority requesting suspension must appear and prove the grounds for permanent revocation of the license. (5) Failure of the requesting authority to appear at the hearing may cause reinstatement of license to licensee."

158   IC 35-47-2-5(b) (documented evidence that a person is not now a "proper person" is grounds for immediate suspension or revocation of license).

159   IC 35-47-2-5(d) (Superintendent shall establish rules concerning the procedure for suspending or revoking a person's license).

160   240 IAC 3-1-1 through 3-4-1.

161   240 IAC 3-2-1(1) (Superintendent will suspend a license upon written

request of police agency).

162   *See* 240 IAC 3-2-1(2) (written request must state reasonable grounds for suspension).

163   240 IAC 3-2-1(3) (notice and right to immediate hearing).

164   240 IAC 3-2-1(4) (authority requesting suspension must appear).

165   240 IAC 3-2-1(5) (failure of requesting authority to appear for administrative hearing may cause reinstatement).

166   The administrative rule is 240 IAC 3-3-1, which provides: "(1) The Superintendent will permanently revoke a license only if he has proof of the allegation which served as the grounds for the temporary suspension."

167   IC 4-21.5-1-1, *et seq.* (administrative proceedings regarding licenses).

168   The author has worked on several such cases and given the right facts and circumstances, even a permanent revocation can be vacated and a license re-instated. Counsel addressing such a matter should first start with a call to the Firearms Section of the Indiana State Police. They are always very helpful.

169   IC 35-47-2-20 (statute on removal of a disability).

170   IC 35-47-2-21(b) (foreign handgun permits recognized by Indiana as valid).

171   Under strict reciprocity doctrine, Indiana would not recognize state X's handgun license if they did not recognize Indiana's handgun license. However, as a practical matter, this doctrine has become diluted. In Indiana, for instance, the state recognizes all foreign states' permits, regardless of whether they recognize Indiana's permits. Thus, it is the case in fact, that other states' permits are recognized as valid by Indiana law, allowing their residents to carry a handgun in Indiana, but the "reciprocal" state does not recognize Indiana's licenses.

172   Typically, reciprocity comes into law in one of two ways. First, a state legislature may enact a statute recognizing all foreign permits. Second, a legislature may empower the state attorney general, under certain circumstances, to enter into compacts for state-to-state carry.

173   *See generally Santini v. Consolidated Rail Corporation*, 505 N.E.2d 832, 835-56 (Ind.Ct.App. 1987) (under the supremacy clause and commerce clause of the Constitution, the Congress could nullify state and local laws that are contrary to federal law, and the Congress is authorized to absolutely preempt state and local rulemaking authority in a particular field, but it does not have to do so).

174   The author believes that based on his following on federal campaigns for national licensing, this is likely to never pass and become law, at least for civilians without police powers. *See generally American Handgunner*, "Speakout" (March/April 2004), p. 8 (topic is the subject of heated debate even among the "pro-gun" lobby as to who would be included within any such national license).

175   The Legislature's preemption statute on local firearms regulation is codified at IC 35-47-11-2, which provides: "Notwithstanding IC 36-1-3, a [political] unit may not regulate in any manner the ownership, possession, sale, transfer, or transportation of firearms (as defined in IC 35-47-1-5) or ammunition except as follows: (1) This chapter does not apply to land, buildings, or other real property owned or administered by a unit, except highways (as defined in IC 8-23-1-23) or public highways (as defined in IC 8-2.1-17-14). (2) Notwithstanding the limitation in this section, a unit may use the unit's planning and zoning powers under IC 36-7-4 to prohibit the sale of firearms within two hundred (200) feet of a school by a person having a business that did not sell firearms within two hundred (200) feet of a school before April 1, 1994. (3) Notwithstanding the limitation in this section, a legislative body of a unit other than a township may adopt an emergency ordinance or a unit other than a township may take other action allowed under section 6 of this chapter to regulate the sale of firearms anywhere within the unit for a period of not more than seventy-two (72) hours after the regulatory action takes effect."

176   IC 35-47-2-21(b) (Indiana's handgun license reciprocity statute).

177   *See also* J. Scott Kappas, *Traveler's Guide to the Firearms Laws of the*

Fifty States (2004 ed.). This guide is available from "www.gunlawguide.com".

178   Under Alabama statutory law, citizens from other states may legally carry their handguns in Alabama, so long as they have a valid handgun permit in their home state and their home state allows reciprocity for Alabama residents as determined by the Alabama Attorney General. This reciprocity provision extends to Indiana licensees, and the Alabama Attorney General has specifically recognized Indiana's license. The Alabama Office of the Attorney General provides an excellent on-line summary of Alabama handgun law, and can be found at the following cite: "www.ago.state.al.us". The specific Alabama statute on reciprocity is § 13A-11-85, which provides: "(a) A person licensed to carry a handgun in any state whose laws recognize and give effect in that state to a license issued under the laws of the State of Alabama shall be authorized to carry a handgun in this state. This section shall apply to a licenseholder from another state only while the licenseholder is not a resident of this state. A licenseholder from another state shall carry the handgun in compliance with the laws of this state. (b) The Attorney General shall periodically publish a list of states which meet the requirements of subsection (a)."

179   Pursuant to Alaska law, a citizen of another state holding a handgun carry license issued under his/her state of domicile, can validly carry in Alaska. Information about Alaska carry may be obtained form the Alaska Department of Public Safety website at "www.dps.state.ak.us". The specific Alaska statute is section 18.65.748, which provides: "A person holding a valid permit to carry a concealed handgun from another state or a political subdivision of another state is a permittee under [Alaska law]."

180   On March 18, 2003, Colorado Governor Bill Owens signed into a law SB24, which is codified at CRS 18-12-213. This statute directs that Colorado will recognize a valid permit issued in another state if the permittee is 21 years of age and the other state recognizes Colorado permits as valid in their state. Indiana's statute clearly allows a Colorado permit to be valid for carry. The Colorado Bureau of Investigation has recognized Indiana's handgun permit as valid in Colorado. More information may be obtained from the Colorado Bureau of Investigation's website: "http://www.cbi.state.co.us/ccw/reciprocity.asp"

181   With the addition of Florida Statute 709.015 in 1999, the Florida Division of Licensing, Florida Department of Agriculture and Consumer Services, was empowered to enter into reciprocal agreements with other states on the issue of

carrying concealed weapons. Several states have entered into such reciprocal agreements with Florida. Indiana has a pact with Florida. The premier work on Florida is enumerated in the Preface footnotes of this Book. The Florida statutory scheme for reciprocity provides: "(1) Notwithstanding s. 790.01, a resident of the United States who is a nonresident of Florida may carry a concealed weapon or concealed firearm while in this state if the nonresident: (a) Is 21 years of age or older; and (b) Has in his or her immediate possession a valid license to carry a concealed weapon or concealed firearm issued to the nonresident in his or her state of residence."

182   The Georgia statute is a standard reciprocity statute and is codified at § 16-11-126(e). Additional information about reciprocity may be obtained from the Department of Law, State of Georgia, Attorney General, through its website at "www.state.ga.us/ago". This statute provides: "On and after October 1, 1996, a person licensed to carry a handgun in any state whose laws recognize and give effect within such state to a license issued pursuant to this part shall be authorized to carry a handgun in this state, but only while the licensee is not a resident of this state; provided, however, that such licenseholder shall carry the handgun in compliance with the laws of this state."

183   The Idaho statutory scheme allows concealed carry of a handgun with an Indiana license under Idaho Code § 18-3302(12)(g). This statute provides: "(12) The requirement to secure a license to carry a concealed weapon under this section shall not apply to the following persons: . . . .(g) Any person who has a valid permit from a state or local law enforcement agency or court authorizing him to carry a concealed weapon. A permit issued in another state will only be considered valid if the permit is in the licensee's physical possession."

184   Kentucky allows all persons possessing a handgun permit of another state to carry in Kentucky. Information about restrictions and limitations may be obtained from the Kentucky Coalition to Carry Concealed at their website at "www.kc3.com". The concealed carry statute is pursuant to Kentucky Revised Statute 237.110(17)(a). This statute provides: "A person who has a valid license issued by another state of the United States to carry a concealed deadly weapon in that state may, subject to the provisions of Kentucky law, carry a concealed weapon in Kentucky, and his license shall be considered as valid in Kentucky."

185   The State of Michigan, through legislative act, and enactment in its

statutory code, the Michigan Compiled Laws § 28.432a(f), recognizes foreign permits. Information may be obtained from the Michigan Department of Attorney General at "www.michigan.gov/ag". The reciprocity statute provides: "The requirements of this act for obtaining a license to carry a concealed pistol do not apply to any of the following . . . . (f) A resident of another state who is licensed by that state to carry a concealed pistol."

186   The State of Montana recognizes handgun permits from other states if the: (1) state issued in requires criminal background checks; (2) the permit is in holder's possession; and the (3) permit holder has photo identification. The Montana Attorney General has recognized Indiana as a state that so complies. Such acknowledgment and state firearms law can be found on the Montana Department of Justice's website: "www.doj.state.mt.us".

187   New Hampshire also recognizes Indiana's license because Indiana recognizes New Hampshire's handgun permits pursuant to New Hampshire Revised Statute § 159:6-d. This statute provides: "Notwithstanding the provisions of RSA 159:6, no nonresident holding a current and valid license to carry a loaded pistol or revolver in the state in which he resides or who is a peace officer in the state in which he resides, shall be required to obtain a license to carry a loaded pistol or revolver within this state if: I. Such nonresident carries upon his person the license held from the state in which he resides; and II. The state in which such person is a resident provides a reciprocal privilege for residents of this state."

188   One of the frequently asked questions on the Oklahoma Attorney General's website is, "Is my out-of-state concealed weapon permit valid when I travel through Oklahoma?" The answer for Indiana licensees is "Yes", because Indiana recognizes Oklahoma's permittees. Additional information may be obtained from the Oklahoma Attorney General's website at "www.oag.state.ok.us". Oklahoma Statute Title 21, § 1290.26 is the relevant provision. This statute provides: "The State of Oklahoma hereby recognizes any valid concealed carry weapons permit or license issued by another state, provided the issuing state recognizes this state's concealed handgun license and the reciprocal state... Any person entering this state in possession of a firearm authorized for concealed carry upon the authority of a reciprocal state is authorized to continue to carry a concealed firearm in this state; provided the firearm remains fully concealed from detection and view, and that upon coming in contact with any peace officer of this state, the person discloses the fact that he or she is in possession of a concealed firearm pursuant to a valid

concealed carry weapons permit or license issued by another state."

189   Pursuant to SDCL 23-2-7.3, the Attorney General and the Secretary of State can enter into reciprocity agreements with other states, and Indiana is such a state.   South Dakota has an official state publication titled *2003 South Dakota Firearms Law Booklet* summarizing various handgun laws of the state. Additional information is available through the Secretary of State's web site at "www.state.sd.us".   The statute provides: "The attorney general shall compare South Dakota permit issuance statutes with the permit issuance statutes in states with which reciprocity is sought or requested in order to determine whether the laws of the other state meet or exceed the requirements of this chapter for the issuance of a permit. The secretary of state may enter into reciprocity agreements with other states after the attorney general has notified the secretary of state that the other states' laws meet or exceed the provisions of this chapter."

190   The State of Tennessee by statute, Tennessee Code 39-17-1351(r)(1)(2), recognizes foreign permits. Additional information is available on the Tennessee Firearms Association's website at "www.tennesseefirearms.com".   This statute provides: "(r)(1) A facially valid handgun permit, firearms permit, weapons permit or license issued by another state shall be valid in this state according to its terms and shall be treated as if it is a handgun permit issued by this state; provided, however, the provisions of this subsection (r) shall not be construed to authorize the holder of any out-of-state permit or license to carry, in this state, any firearm or weapon other than a handgun. (2) For a person to lawfully carry a handgun in this state based upon a permit or license issued in another state, the person must be in possession of the permit or license at all times such person carries a handgun in this state."

191   Utah's Concealed Weapons Act, codified at Utah Code Annotated § 76-10-523, which prohibits the carrying of a handgun and makes such carry a criminal act, excepts from its scope any person issued a license by another state. This statute provides: "(2) The provisions of Subsections 76-10-504(1)(a), (1)(b), and Section 76-10-505 do not apply to any person to whom a permit to carry a concealed firearm has been issued: . . . .(b) by another state or county".

192   Vermont does not require licensing of any type to carry a concealed or openly carried handgun. However, there is statutory regulation insofar as it relates

to the intent of carrying the weapon under Vermont Statutes Annotated, 13 V.S.A. § 4003. This statute provides: " A person who carries a dangerous or deadly weapon, openly or concealed, with the intent or avowed purpose of injuring a fellow man, or who carries a dangerous or deadly weapon within any state institution or upon the grounds or lands owned or leased for the use of such institution, without the approval of the warden or Superintendent of the institution, shall be imprisoned not more than two years or fined not more than $200.00, or both."

193   Wyoming has reciprocity with other states that recognize Wyoming's handgun permits, but only if the reciprocal state has laws, including those on background checks, that are similar to Wyoming's laws. The Wyoming Attorney General makes this determination, and has recognized Indiana's handgun licenses thereunder. The Wyoming Attorney General also provides substantial background information about Wyoming firearms law at "attorneygeneral.state.wy.us". The relevant statutory provision is Wyoming Statute § 6-8-104(a)(iii). This statute provides: "(a) A person who wears or carries a concealed deadly weapon is guilty of a misdemeanor . . .unless (iii) The person holds a valid permit authorizing him to carry a concealed firearm authorized and issued by a governmental agency or entity in another state that recognizes Wyoming permits, is a valid statewide permit, and the state has laws similar to the provisions of this section, as determined by the attorney general, including a proper background check of the permit holder."

194   *See* Chapters 4 through 13 (covering many of the substantial Indiana and federal restrictions to carrying of a handgun).

195   *See generally* IC 35-44-3-9 (prohibiting handguns and other weapons in jails); IC 35-47-9-2 (prohibiting handguns and other weapons at schools); IC 35-47-6-1 (prohibiting handguns and other weapons on commercial or chartered aircraft); IC 35-47-6-1.3 (prohibiting handguns and other weapons in controlled access areas of airports and on airplanes).

196   *See generally* IC 35-47-2-1, *et seq.* (handgun license statutes).

197   *See* Chapters 4 through 13 (covering many of the substantial Indiana and federal restrictions to carrying of a handgun with a license).

198   IC 35-47-4-3 (pointing firearm at another person is a crime).

199   IC 35-47-9-2 (prohibiting handguns and other weapons on school grounds, at schools, on school buses, and at school functions).

200   *See* Chapters 4 through 6 (Indiana statutory carry restrictions).

201   *See* Chapters 7 through 9 (Indiana administrative restrictions; federal restrictions are only cited briefly herein because they generally overlap with federal statutory property restrictions).

202   *See* Chapter 10 (Indiana courthouse and courtroom restrictions).

203   *See* Chapters 11 through 12 (federal statutory restrictions).

204   *See* Chapter 13 (private property restrictions).

205   The statute defining what constitutes a "penal facility" is codified at IC 35-41-1-21, which provides: "'Penal facility' means state prison, correctional facility, county jail, penitentiary, house of correction, or any other facility for confinement of persons under sentence, or awaiting trial or sentence, for offenses. The term includes a correctional facility constructed under IC 4-13.5."

206   *See generally* Wayne R. LaFave & Austin W. Scott, Jr., *Criminal Law* §1.2 (2nd ed. 1986) (excellent discussion of the purposes of criminal law and mortality and criminal law).

207   Comprehensive criminal corrections statistics are found on the U.S. Department of Justice's website at "http://www.ojp.usdoj.gov/bjs/correction.htm".

208   While beyond the scope of this Book, there are substantial administrative regulations in this area. These can be referenced through Title 210 of the IAC, which is the provision of the IAC covering the Department of Corrections. For example, 210 IAC 3-1-7 addresses criteria for the physical plant and mandates weapons storage and related issues. Further, 210 IAC 3-1-13 requires that each county sheriff have a manual addressing numerous jail-safety issues, including provisions relating to firearms, such as prohibiting the taking of firearms past

designated secured areas.

209   *Id.*

210   The statute that prohibits trafficking with an inmate is IC 35-44-3-9, which provides: "(a) As used in this section, 'juvenile facility' means the following: (1) A secure facility (as defined in IC 31-9-2-114) in which a child is detained under IC 31 or used for a child awaiting adjudication or adjudicated under IC 31 as a child in need of services or a delinquent child. (2) A shelter care facility (as defined in IC 31-9-2-117) in which a child is detained under IC 31 or used for a child awaiting adjudication or adjudicated under IC 31 as a child in need of services or a delinquent child. (b) A person who, without the prior authorization of the person in charge of a penal or juvenile facility knowingly or intentionally: (1) delivers, or carries into the penal facility or juvenile facility with the intent to deliver, an article to an inmate or child of the facility; (2) carries, or receives with intent to carry out of the penal facility or juvenile facility, an article from an inmate or child of the facility; or (3) delivers, or carries to a work site with the intent to deliver, alcoholic beverages to an inmate or a child of a jail work crew or community work crew; commits trafficking with an inmate, a Class A misdemeanor. However, the offense is a Class C felony if the article is a controlled substance or deadly weapon."

211   *Id.*

212   *Id.*

213   *Id.*

214   The term "deadly weapon" is codified at IC 35-41-1-8, which provides: "'Deadly weapons' means the following: (1) A loaded or unloaded firearm. (2) A destructive device, weapon, device, taser (as defined in IC 35-47-8-3) or electronic stun weapon (as defined in IC 35-47-8-1), equipment, chemical substance, or other material that in the manner it is used, or could ordinarily be used, or is intended to be used, is readily capable of causing serious bodily injury. (3) An animal (as defined in IC 35-46-3-3) that is: (A) readily capable of causing serious bodily injury; and (B) used in the commission or attempted commission of a crime. (4) A biological disease, virus, or organism that is capable of causing serious bodily injury."

215   IC 35-44-3-9 (trafficking with an inmate crime enhanced if deadly weapon).

216   This is as opposed to quasi-criminal acts, such a probation revocation, which is governed by a civil, preponderance of the evidence, standard.

217   *See, e.g., Powers v. State*, 540 N.E.2d 1225, 1227 (Ind. 1989) (burden of proving all elements of a criminal offense beyond a reasonable doubt rests with the prosecution).

218   *See, e.g., Brown v. State*, 485 N.E.2d 108, 111 (Ind. 1985) (defendant has burden of proof on any affirmative defense).

219   The intentional or knowingly carrying of a deadly weapon into the facility, with the intent to deliver to an inmate, is an element of the crime--the mental or intent element. Failure of the prosecution to prove this beyond a reasonable doubt, negates an element of the crime being established and requires acquittal. This is a highly technical area , and is often referred to as the *mens rea* element of the crime, although some crimes may be committed without intent. *See generally Concepcion v. State*, 796 N.E.2d 1256, 1261 (Ind.Ct.App. 2003) (*mens rea* ranges from specific intent, to a less severe culpable mental state, such as "knowingly" or "recklessly").

220   This is the author's experience at most jail-type facilities visited in the scope of meeting with incarcerated clients.

221   *See, e.g., Hoffman v. State*, 520, N.E.2d 436, 438 (Ind. 1988) (prosecution may use surrounding circumstances, for example, and inferences to show criminal intent).

222   The author can distinctly remember being in a licensed shelter care facility, where a child of an international parental abduction was being held, pending transportation back to Africa. Aside from jurisdiction issues, this was a CHINS child, and this exception would have applied. The home did not look like a jail facility. Thus, the license holder must constantly filter her/her daily actions while carrying in order to comply with the law. Carry is a big responsibility, and

requires such thoughtful consideration on an on-going basis.

223   *See* IC 35-44-3-9(b) (allows prior authorization to bring in what would be contraband in proper circumstances).

224   The sentence for a Class C Felony is IC 35-50-2-6, which provides: "(a) A person who commits a Class C felony shall be imprisoned for a fix term of four (4) years, with not more than four (4) years added for aggravating circumstances or not more than two (2) years subtracted for mitigating circumstances. In addition, he may be fined not more than ten thousand dollars ($10,000.00)."

225   *See* the statutory history (added by Acts 1976, P.L.148, SEC.4. Amended by Acts 1977,P.L.340, SEC.67; Acts 1981, P.L.300, SEC.2; P.L.223-1996, SEC.1.).

226   *See* the statutory history (amended by P.L. 183-1999, SEC.2; P.L.243-1999, SEC.2.).

227   IC 35-41-1-21 (definition of penal facility).

228   *Id.*

229   This is determined by tracing the various statutory empowerments to construct penal-type facilities, beginning with IC 35-41-1-21.

230   IC 35-44-3-9 (trafficking statute).

231   The statute defining a "secure facility" is IC 31-9-2-114, which provides: "'Secure facility', for purposes of the juvenile law, means a place of residence, other than a shelter care facility, that prohibits the departure of a child."

232   The statute defining a "shelter care facility" is IC 31-9-2-117, which provides: "'Shelter care facility', for purposes of the juvenile law, means a place of residence that: (1) is licensed under the laws of any state; and (2) is not locked to prevent a child's departure unless the administrator determines that locking is

necessary to protect the child's health."

233   The statutory definition of a "prison" is codified at 18 U.S.C. § 1791(F)(4), which provides: "(4) the term 'prison' means a Federal correctional, detention, or penal facility."

234   The statutory definition of the relevant "prohibited item" is codified at 18 U.S.C. § 1791(d)(1)(A), which provides: "(d) Definitions. As used in this section (1) the term 'prohibited object' means– (A) a firearm or destructive device or controlled substance in schedule I or II, other than marijuana or a controlled substance referred to in subparagraph (C) of this subsection[.]"

235   This criminal statute regarding transporting prohibited articles into a federal prison is codified at 18 U.S.C. § 1791(a), which provides: "(a) Offense. Whoever (1) in violation of a statute or rule or order issued under a statute, provides to an inmate of a prison a prohibited object, or attempts to do so; or (2) being an inmate of a prison, makes, possesses, or obtains, or attempts to make or obtain, a prohibited object; shall be punished as provided in subsection (b) of this section."

236   The punishment for taking, or attempting to take, a prohibited item, namely a firearm, to an inmate at a federal prison is codified at 18 U.S.C. § 1791(b)(2), which provides: "(b) Punishment.–   The punishment for an offense under this section is a fine under this title or– . . . .(2) imprisonment for not more than 10 years, or both, if the object is specified in subsection (d)(1)(A) of this section[.]"

237   Information about the April 21, 1999, school shootings at Columbine High School, in Colorado, can be obtained from CNN.com.

238   In Article 47, the term "firearm" is defined as a "handgun", making it clear that a firearm is the genus, and the handgun is a species thereof, and hence, included within the prohibition. The statutory inclusion language and definitions are codified at IC35-47-1-1, which provides: "The definitions in this chapter apply throughout this article."

239   The statute that precludes possession of firearms at schools, school

functions, and on school buses is IC 35-47-9-2, which provides: "A person who possesses a firearm: (1) in or on school property; (2) in or on property that is being used by a school for a school function; (3) or on a school bus; commits a Class D felony."

240   The term "firearm" is defined in IC 35-47-1-5, which provides: "'Firearm' means any weapon that is capable of or designed to or that may readily be converted to expel a projectile by means of an explosion."

241   The term "handgun" is defined in IC 35-47-1-6, which provides: "'Handgun' means any firearm: (1) designed or adapted so as to be aimed and fired from one (1) hand, regardless of barrel length; or (2) any firearm with: (A) a barrel less than sixteen (16) inches in length; or (B) an overall length of less than twenty-six (26) inches."

242   *See P.L.140-1994, SEC.11* (public law creating prohibition of firearms at schools).

243   *See French v. State*, 778 N.E.2d 816, 823 (Ind. 2002) (pre-school operated by church is private school property).

244   IC 35-47-9-2 (statutory prohibition of firearms at schools).

245   The statute creating this affirmative defense and exemptions from the prohibition of firearms at school is codified at IC 35-47-9-1, which provides: "This chapter does not to apply to the following (1) A: (A) federal; (B) state; or (C) local; law enforcement officer. (2) A person who has been employed or authorized by: (A) a school; or (B) another person who owns or operates property being used by a school for a school function; to act as a security guard, perform or participate in a school function, or participate in any other activity authorized by a school. (3) A person who: (A) may legally possess a firearm; and (B) possesses the firearm in a motor vehicle that is being operated by the person to transport another person to or from a school or a school function."

246   IC 35-47-9-1 (persons excluded from criminal prohibition of firearms at schools).

247   IC 35-47-9-2 (statutory prohibition of firearms at schools).

248   *See Harris v. State,* 716 N.E.2d 406, 411 (Ind. 1999) (state must prove beyond a reasonable doubt that the defendant carried a handgun on or about his person, away from his dwelling or business, and thereafter, the burden is in on the defendant).

249   Criminal strict liability refers narrowly to those penal statutes that contain no intent, or *mens rea*, element at all. *See Walker v. Indiana,* 668 N.E.2d 243, 245 (Ind. 1996).

250   IC 35-47-9-1(2) (affirmative defense to carry of a firearm if authorized by the school for security purposes or by the facility where the event is occurring).

251   IC 35-47-9-1(3) (affirmative defense for possession of a handgun with Indiana permit, if while operating vehicle and dropping off or picking up someone at school).

252   *Id.*

253   *See Newson* , 785 N.E.2d at 1155 (establishing the school drop-off/pick-up language of the statute as an affirmative defense). Selected text from the *Newson* opinion is as follows: ". . .on November 6, 2001, a student at Ben Davis High School in Indianapolis noticed a handgun in the passenger seat of a car parked by the service dock and reported it to school officials. Principal David Marcotte verified the report and notified school security. School security officer James Ingalls opened the car door and retrieved the handgun. Shortly thereafter, Newson approached the car, acknowledged ownership of the vehicle and the handgun, and produced a valid Indiana gun permit. The state charged Newson with possession of firearms on school property, a Class D felony. On May 3, 2002, the trial court found Newson guility as charged [even though Newson raised having this in his auto as an affirmative defense under the statute]... It is undisputed that Newson legally possessed the handgun; at issue is whether he possessed it in a motor vehicle 'that [was] being operated' to transport another person to the school. Ind.Code 35-47-9-1(3). The record clearly indicates that Newson was not operating his car when the student saw the handgun in the passenger seat. As such, we must conclude that Newson failed to establish his affirmative defense. Affirmed."

254   That sentencing statute for a Class D felony is IC 35-50-2-7, which provides: "(a) A person who commits a Class D felony shall be imprisoned for a fixed term of one and one-half (1 ½) years, with not more than one and one-half (1 ½) years added for aggravating circumstances or not more than one (1) year subtracted for mitigating circumstances. In addition, he may be fined not more than ten thousand dollars ($10,000)."

255   *See generally* IC 35-47-9-1 and 35-47-9-2 (no definition of the term "school property" in these statutes).

256   The term "school property" is defined in IC 35-41-1-24.7, which provides: "'School property' means the following: (1) A building or other structure owned or rented by: (A) a school corporation; (B) an entity that is required to be licensed under IC 12-17.2 or IC 12-17.4; (C) a private school (as defined in IC 20-9.1-1-3); or (D) a federal, state, local, or nonprofit program or service operated to serve, assist, or otherwise benefit children who are at least three (3) years of age and not yet enrolled in kindergarten, including the following: (i) A Head Start program under 42 U.S.C. 9831 et seq. (ii) A special education preschool program. (iii) A developmental child care program for preschool children. (2) The grounds adjacent to and owned or rented in common with a building or other structure described in subdivision (1)."

257   Title 35, Article 41, enumerates substantive criminal provisions, and begins with definitions, including the definition of "school property" and "school bus", which IC 35-41-1-3 specifically applies to the entire penal code.

258   *See Newson,* 785 N.E. 2d at 1158 (statute on exceptions to guns at school prohibition creates an affirmative defense for drop-offs/pick-ups from school in certain narrow factual contexts).

259   This statute defining a "school corporation", IC 20-9.1-1-1, provides: "Definition, 'School Corporation'. As used in this article, the term 'school corporation' means any public school corporation established by and under the laws of the state of Indiana. The term includes, but is not necessarily limited to, any school city, school town, school township, consolidated school corporation, metropolitan school district, township school corporation, county school corporation, united school corporation or any community school corporation."

260   IC 12-17.4, referenced in the "school property" definition, as an entity included therein, encompasses licensed residential child care establishments.

261   IC 12-17.2, referenced in the "school property" definition, as an entity included therein, encompasses licensed day care facilities.

262   IC 20-9.1-1-3, referenced in the "school property" definition, as a type of included school, encompasses a defined "private school." This definition provides: "Definition, 'Private School'.   As used in this article, the term 'private school' means any school which is not supported and maintained by funds realized from the imposition of tax on property, income or sales tax."

263   IC 35-41-1-24.7(1)(D)(i)(ii)(iii).

264   IC 35-41-1-24.7(1)(2) (school property includes building or other structure owned or rented by included school entities, plus the grounds adjacent to and owned or rented in common with these structures).

265   *See French,* 778 N.E. 2d at 823 (term "school property" includes church with a kindergarten).

266   IC 35-47-9-1(3) (affirmative defense does not encompass the factual scenario of properly stowing handgun within a vehicle on school property).

267   The statute precluding firearms at "schools", IC 35-47-9-2, and definition of "school property" are silent as to whether they encompass post-secondary education.   No Indiana case has passed on this issue.

268   While an unanswered question of post-secondary schools being included under the state school firearm provision, this is not the case under federal law respecting weapons in school zones.   This is because a "school" is an elementary or secondary school under federal law pursuant to 18 U.S.C. § 921(a)(26), which provides: "The term 'school' means a school which provides elementary or secondary education, as determined under state law."

269   The term "school bus" for purposes of the penal code is enumerated in IC 35-41-1-24.3, and provides: "'School bus' means any motor vehicle designed and constructed for the accommodation of more than ten (10) passengers, which is used for the transportation of Indiana school children."

270   The term "special purpose bus" for purposes of the educational and penal code is enumerated in IC 20-9.1-1-4.5, provides: "Definition, 'Special Purpose Bus'. As used in this article, the term 'special purpose bus' means any motor vehicle designed and constructed for the accommodation of more than six (6) passengers, and used by a school corporation for transportation purposes not appropriate for school buses."

271   *See* IC 35-41-1-1 through 35-41-1-29.4 (definitions applicable to the criminal code, with no definition of "school function"); *see also* IC 20-9.1-1-1 through 20-9.1-1-12 (definitions applicable to elementary and secondary education, with no definition of "school function").

272   This rule is codified in IC 1-1-4-1, which provides: "The construction of all statutes of this state shall be by the following rules, unless the construction is plainly repugnant to the intent of the legislature or of the context of the statute: (1) Words and phrases shall be taken in their plain, or ordinary and usual, sense. Technical words and phrases having a peculiar and appropriate meaning in law shall be understood according to their technical import. . . ."

273   *See, e.g., Stratton,* 791 N.E.2d at 224 (courts may consult English language dictionaries to ascertain the plain and ordinary meaning of a statutory term).

274   *Merriam-Webster's Collegiate Dictionary Tenth Edition* at 471 (2001).

275   The statute defining "school zone" is 18 § USC 921(25), and provides: "(25) The term 'school zone' means (A) in, or on the grounds of, a public, parochial or private school; or (B) within a distance of 1,000 feet from the grounds of a public, parochial or private school."

276   This power to enact criminal laws regarding guns in school zones was determined by a Congressional finding that is codified at 18 U.S.C. § 922, which

provides: "(q)(1) The Congress finds and declares that (I) the Congress has the power, under the interstate commerce clause and other provisions of the Constitution, to enact measures to ensure the integrity and safety of the Nation's schools by enactment of this subsection."

277   The federal statute precluding possession of firearms in school zones is 18 U.S.C. § 922(q)(2)(A), which provides: "It shall be unlawful for any individual knowingly to possess a firearm that has moved in or that otherwise affects interstate or foreign commerce at a place that the individual knows, or has reasonable cause to believe is a school zone."

278   The statutory exceptions for carrying a handgun within "school zone" are codified at 18 U.S.C. 922(q)(2)(B), which provides: "Subparagraph (A) does not apply to the possession of a firearm (i) on private property not part of school grounds; (ii) if the individual possessing the firearm is licensed to do so by the State in which the school zone is located or a political subdivision of the State, and the law of the State or political subdivision requires that, before an individual obtains such a license, the law enforcement authorities of the State or political subdivision verify that the individual is qualified under law to receive the license; (iii) that is (I) not loaded; and (II) in a locked container, or a locked firearms rack that is on a motor vehicle; (iv) by an individual for use in a program approved by a school in the school zone; (v) by an individual in accordance with a contract entered into between a school in the school zone and the individual or an employer of the individual; (vi) by a law enforcement officer acting in his or her official capacity; or (vii) that is unloaded and is possessed by an individual while traversing school premises for the purpose of gaining access to public or private lands open to hunting, if the entry on school premises is authorized by school authorities."

279   The statutory punishment scheme for violating federal criminal laws with regard to firearms in a school zone is codified at 18 U.S.C. 924(a)(4), and provides: "Whoever violates section 922(q) shall be fined under this title, imprisoned for not more than 5 years, or both. Notwithstanding any other provision of law, the term of imprisonment imposed under this paragraph shall not run concurrently with any other term of imprisonment imposed under any other provision of law. Except for the authorization of a term of imprisonment of not more than 5 years made in this paragraph, for the purpose of any other law a violation of section 922(q) shall be deemed to be a misdemeanor."

280   The statute prohibiting firearms at and beyond a controlled area of an airport is IC 35-47-6-1.3, and provides: "A person who knowingly or intentionally enters an area of an airport to which access is controlled by the inspection of persons and property while the person: (1) possesses: (A) a firearm; (B) an explosive; or (C) any other deadly weapon; or (2) has access to property that contains: (A) a firearm; (B) an explosive; or (C) any other deadly weapon; commits a Class A misdemeanor."

281   The statute prohibiting a person from boarding a flight with a handgun is IC 35-47-6-1, and provides: "A person who boards a commercial or charter aircraft having in his possession: (1) a firearm; (2) an explosive; or (3) any other deadly weapon; commits a Class C felony."

282   The statute excepting firearms possession at and beyond controlled areas of an airport, or on an aircraft, is codified at IC 35-47-6-0.5, and provides: "(a) Except as provided in subsection (b), this chapter does not apply to an official or employee: (1) of: (A) the United States; (B) a state or political subdivision of a state; (C) an operator (as defined in IC 5-23-2-8); or (D) any other entity that has been granted statutory authority to enforce the penal laws of Indiana;(2) who has been granted the power to effect arrests under Indiana law; and (3) who has been authorized by the official's or employee's agency or employer to carry firearms. (b) An individual described in subsection (a) is subject to the applicable regulation of the United States concerning the possession and carriage of firearms on aircraft or in areas of an airport to which access is controlled by the inspection of persons and property."

283   IC 35-47-6-1 (prohibition against boarding flight with handgun).

284   IC 35-47-6-1.3 (prohibition against taking handgun at and beyond controlled point of airport).

285   IC 35-47-6-1 (prohibition against taking handgun onto aircraft).

286   IC 35-47-6-1.3 (prohibition against taking handgun at and beyond controlled point of airport).

287   *See, e.g., Pope v. State*, 737 N.E.2d 374, 381 (Ind. 2000) (criminal

standard of beyond a reasonable doubt).

288   *See State v. Shelton,* 692 N.E.2d 947, 950 (Ind.Ct.App. 1998) (finding that criminal statute did not have *mens rea* element, meaning that prosecution's showing did not require any culpable mental state).

289   *See State v. Keihn,* 542 N.E.2d 963, 965-66 (Ind. 1989) (General Assembly can vary or eliminate culpable mental state, although generally criminal intent has been viewed as a presumptive element in criminal offenses).

290   *See Hevenor v. State,* 784 N.E.2d 937, 941 (Ind.Ct.App. 2003) (strict liability offenses are not unknown to criminal law and do not invariably offend constitutional requirements).

291   *See Thompson v. State,* 646 N.E.2d 687, 692 (Ind.Ct.App. 1995) (discussion of the permissible use of inferences in criminal cases).

292   The sentence for a Class C Felony is codified at IC 35-50-2-6, and provides: "(a) A person who commits a Class C felony shall be imprisoned for a fixed term of four (4) years, with not more than four (4) years added for aggravating circumstances or not more than two (2) years subtracted for mitigating circumstances. In addition, he may be fined not more than ten thousand dollars ($10,000.00)."

293   IC 35-47-2-23 (crimes and punishment for handgun violations).

294   The statute creating the State Fair Commission is IC 15-1.5-2-1, and provides: "The state fair commission is established. The commission is a separate body, corporate and politic. The commission is not a state agency. The commission performs essential governmental functions."

295   The duty to develop the fairgrounds is by statute at IC 15-1.5-3-1, and provides: "The commission shall maintain and develop the fairgrounds and other property owned by the commission."

296   The State Fair Commission's administrative rule prohibiting deadly

weapons at the annual state fair is at 80 IAC 4-4-4, and provides: "(a) This rule does not apply to a federal, state, or local law enforcement officer or to a person who has been employed or authorized by the state fair commission to provide security protection and services during the annual state fair. (b) No person in possession of a deadly weapon shall be permitted onto or be permitted to remain on the fairgrounds during the annual state fair. (c) Any deadly weapon found in the possession of a person while on the fairgrounds during the annual state fair is subject to immediate confiscation by law enforcement officers or other persons authorized by the executive director of the state fair commission.(d) Any person properly licensed to carry a firearm must secure the firearm in a locked compartment of his or her vehicle, and it shall not be visible to passerby."

297   *Id.*

298   80 IAC 4-4-4(b) (no person in possession of a deadly weapon shall be permitted at the annual state fair).

299   The Indiana Gaming Commission's administrative rule prohibiting firearms is 68 IAC 1-7-1, and provides: "(a) The following definitions apply throughout this rule (68 IAC 1-7): (1) 'Federal enforcement officer' has the meaning set forth in 5 U.S.C. 8331 or IC 35-41-1-17, or both. (2) 'Law enforcement officer' has the meaning set forth in IC 35-41-1-17. (3) 'Security personnel' means an employee of the riverboat licensee or a supplier licensee who: (A) holds the appropriate level of occupational license under IC 4-33-8 and 68 IAC 2-3; and (B) is employed in the riverboat licensee's security department or by a supplier licensee that contractually provides security services to a riverboat licensee.(b) No individual other than a commission agent shall carry a weapon on board the riverboat during any excursion. A law enforcement officer or a federal enforcement officer whose sole purpose for being on the riverboat is the performance of official duties and who has advised the commission agent or the commission that the officer will be on board the riverboat during an excursion shall be allowed to carry a weapon on board the riverboat during an excursion. (c) The riverboat licensee shall post a sign in a prominent place at the point of passenger ingress stating, 'No weapons are allowed beyond this point. Failure to comply with this rule (68 IAC 1-7) may result in the immediate removal from the riverboat, immediate detention by security personnel, the imposition of civil penalties, or exclusion under IC 4-33'. (d) The riverboat licensee shall provide a secure place to which patrons do not have access to store weapons checked by patrons, off duty

law enforcement officers, or off duty federal enforcement officers. (e) Security personnel may carry a weapon on board the riverboat during times that patrons are not present."

300   Indiana Gaming Commission, Annual Report to the Governor, Fiscal Year 2003, September 1, 2003.

301   68 IAC 1-7-1(b) (no weapons on board the riverboat).

302   68 IAC 1-7-1(c) (Indiana Gaming Commission's administrative rule requiring posting of notice regarding weapons).

303   IC 35-47-2-1(a) (carrying a handgun without a license prohibited except in one's dwelling, property or fixed place of business).

304   68 IAC 1-7-1(d) (riverboat licensee shall provide a secure place to store weapons of patrons).

305   The statutory creation of the Indiana Port Commission is enumerated at IC 8-10-1-1, and provides: "In order to promote the agricultural, industrial and commercial development of the state, and to provide for the general welfare by the construction and operation, in cooperation with the federal government, or otherwise of a modern port system with terminal facilities to accommodate water, rail, truck, air-borne, and other forms of transportation, the Indiana Port Commission is hereby authorized and empowered to construct, maintain and operate, in cooperation with the federal government or otherwise, at such locations as shall be approved by the governor, projects, including without limitation public ports with terminal facilities and traffic exchange points throughout Indiana for all forms of transportation, giving particular attention to the benefits which may accrue to the state and its citizens from all forms of transportation, and to issue revenue bonds of the state payable solely from revenues, to pay the cost of such projects. The commission's powers are not limited to ports and may be exercised throughout Indiana for projects that enhance, foster, aid, provide, or promote economic development, public-private partnerships, and other industrial, commercial, business, and transportation purposes."

306   *Id.*

307   IC 8-10-1-7 (Indiana Port Commission's power to enact administrative rules and regulations comes from the Legislature's powers delegated to same).

308   130 IAC 4-1-1, *et. seq* (Article 4 of the IAC covers port use of Indiana Port Commission ports).

309   The Indiana Port Commission's administrative rule prohibiting concealed weapons is 130 IAC 4-1-7, which provides: "(a) No person except port security, conservation officers, police officers, customs officers, or members of the armed forces of the United States on official duty shall carry firearms, concealed weapons, explosives, or similar inflammable materials on the port area. (b) All persons other than the excepted classes shall: (1) surrender all objects described in subsection (a) to the port security on guard at the entrance gate or to the port director; (2) be given a receipt; and (3) recover the object upon leaving the port area and surrendering the receipt. (c) Shooting anywhere on the port area, either over or on the water or land, within the confines of any port boundary is prohibited without the consent of the port director."

310   *Id.*

311   The Indiana Port Commission has a second administrative rule governing prohibited articles at its ports, 130 IAC 4-1-8, and provides: "No person shall transport or carry on the port property any of the following: (1) alcoholic beverages (excepting, however, alcoholic beverages permitted to be brought into the United States on cruise ships and in course of shipment). (2) Firearms. (3) Weapons. (4) Explosives. (5) Narcotics. (6) Obscene literature."

312   While beyond the scope of this Book, particularly because the licensee cannot carry a handgun on any Indiana Port Commission port under its administrative rules and regulations, the entire statutory scheme regarding ports anticipates federal government involvement. Thus, there may be concurrent federal jurisdiction. *See* IC 8-10-1-1, *et seq.* (statutory scheme empowering the Indiana Port Commission).

313   IC 35-47-2-1(a) (carrying a handgun without a license prohibited except in one's dwelling, property or fixed place of business).

314   The definitions section of the port commission statutory scheme defines "port" at IC 8-10-1-2(b), and provides: "(b) The word 'port' shall include any combination of: (1) any place or places on Lake Michigan, the Ohio River, the Wabash River, or other water bodies, natural or artificial, in which water-borne vessels capable of carrying articles of commerce over navigable bodies of water may be loaded, unloaded or accommodated; and (2) nonmaritime port and traffic exchange points throughout Indiana for the transfer of goods and passengers between all modes of transportation."

315   This was determined by reference to the Ports of Indiana website "www.portsofindiana.com" on January 5, 2004.

316   *As amended by P.L.224-2003 and P.L. 271-2003.*

317   103 IAC 4-1-7(b) (weapons checking provision of the administrative code).

318   *See, e.g.,* Kentucky Revised Statutes Annotated, § 237.110(13) (the newest carry and reciprocal carry statute in Kentucky specifically indicates that "No license issued pursuant to this section shall authorize any person to carry a concealed firearm into . . . .(c) Any courthouse . . . .").

319   The statute allowing a court to make local rules for operation of their court is IC 34-8-1-4, which provides: "Other Indiana courts may establish rules for their own government, supplementary to and not conflicting with the rules prescribed by the supreme court or any statue."

320   *See Indiana Rule of Trial Procedure* 81, which provides: "Each local court may from time to time make and amend rules governing its practice not inconsistent with these rules. In all cases not provided for by rule the local court may regulate its practice in any manner not inconsistent with these rules. Two (2) copies of all rules made by a local court shall upon their promulgation be furnished to the clerk of the Supreme Court and the Court of Appeals."

321   The most readily available compilation source for local rules is the *Indiana Rules of Court* published by Thomson-West and available at 1-800-328-4880. However, only a few counties are published in this reference.

322   Constructive notice is notification of the community at large of a law, fact, or otherwise by mere publication, posting, or the like of same, regardless of whether the individual actually knows of the law or fact. Thus, if a trial court has posted a standing order, but the possessor of an unlimited license is unaware of same, it becomes an open question as to whether a sentence of contempt would stand based on constructive notice. *See generally Plumley v. Stanelle*, 311 N.E.2d 626, 628-630 (Ind.Ct.App. 1974) (discussion of constructive notice).

323   *See Macon v. State*, 629 N.E.2d 883, 885-886 (Ind.Ct.App. 1994) (Ms. Macon apparently had the weapon in her possession in her purse throughout the proceeding in the courtroom, but there was no disruption or disturbance whatever, and therefore direct contempt finding was reversible error); *see also Davis v. State,* 608 N.E.2d 995, 996 (Ind.Ct.App. 1993) (appellant not in direct contempt because although he entered the courthouse with a handgun, it was detected and surrendered before he entered the courtroom).

324   This federal statute regarding firearms in and on federal property is 18 U.S.C. § 930, which provides: "(a) Except as provided in subsection (d), whoever knowingly possesses or causes to be present a firearm or other dangerous weapon in a Federal facility (other than a Federal court facility), or attempts to do so, shall be fined under this title or imprisoned not more than 1 year, or both. (b) Whoever, with intent that a firearm or other dangerous weapon be used in the commission of a crime, knowingly possesses or causes to be present such firearm or dangerous weapon in a Federal facility, or attempts to do so, shall be fined under this title or imprisoned not more than 5 years, or both. (c) A person who kills in the course of a violation of subsection (a) or (b), or in the course of an attack on a Federal facility involving the use of a firearm or other dangerous weapon, or attempts or conspires to do such an act, shall be punished as provided in sections 1111, 1112, 1113, and 1117. (d) Subsection (a) shall not apply to—(1) the lawful performance of official duties by an officer, agent, or employee of the United States, a state, or a political subdivision thereof, who is authorized by law to engage in or supervise prevention, detection, investigation, or prosecution of any violation of law; (2) the possession of a firearm or other dangerous weapon by a Federal official or a member of the Armed Forces if such possession is authorized by law; or (3) the lawful carrying

of firearms or other dangerous weapons in a Federal facility incident to hunting or other lawful purposes. (e)(1) Except as provided in paragraph (2), whoever knowingly possesses or causes to be present a firearm in a Federal court facility, or attempts to do so, shall be fined under this title, imprisoned not more than 2 years, or both. (2) Paragraph (1) shall not apply to conduct which is described in paragraph (1) or (2) of subsection (d). (f) Nothing in this section limits the power of a court of the United States to punish for contempt or to promulgate rules or orders regulating, restricting, or prohibiting the possession of weapons within any building housing such court or any of its proceedings, or upon any grounds appurtenant to such building. (g) As used in this section: (1) The term "Federal facility" means a building or part thereof owned or leased by the Federal Government, where Federal employees are regularly present for the purpose of performing their official duties. (2) The term 'dangerous weapon' means a weapon, device, instrument, material, or substance, animate or inanimate, that is used for, or is readily capable of, causing death or serious bodily injury, except that such term does not include a pocket knife with a blade of less than 2 ½ inches in length. (3) The term "Federal court facility" means the courtroom, judges' chambers, witness rooms, jury deliberation rooms, attorney conference rooms, prisoner holding cells, offices of the court clerks, the United States attorney, and the United States marshal, probation and parole offices, and adjoining corridors of any court of the United States. (h) Notice of the provisions of subsections (a) and (b) shall be posted conspicuously at each public entrance to each Federal facility, and notice of subsection (e) shall be posted conspicuously at each public entrance to each Federal court facility, and no person shall be convicted of an offense under subsection (a) or (e) with respect to a Federal facility if such notice is not so posted at such facility, unless such person had actual notice of subsection (a) or (e), as the case may be."

325   18 U.S.C. § 930(d)(3) (lawful hunting on federal property).

326   18 U.S.C. § 930(d)(1)-(3) (excepted persons from possession of firearms in a federal facility or court).

327   18 U.S.C. § 930(a).

328   18 U.S.C. § 930(a) (incarceration and fines).

329   18 U.S.C. § 930(b) (e)(1) (intended for use in crime in federal facility; knowingly possessing firearm in federal court facility).

330   18 U.S.C. § 930(b) (intended for use in crime in federal facility).

331   18 U.S.C. § 930(e)(1) (knowingly possessing a firearm in a federal court facility).

332   18 U.S.C. § 930(e)(1) (fine and up to two years imprisonment).

333   *See generally* Laurie L. Levenson, *Federal Criminal Rules Handbook* (2003 ed.), P. 287 (standard elements of court instructions for defendant's case in federal cases, including presumption of innocence, reasonable doubt, right to remain silent, intent requirement, standards to evaluate evidence).

334   18 U.S.C. § 930(a)-(e) (intent element of crimes).

335   *See* 18 U.S.C. § 930(h) (conspicuous posting of notice).

336   18 U.S.C. § 930(d)(3) (firearm may be possessed on federal property incident to lawful hunting).

337   Handguns may not be shipped through U.S. mail. They must be lawfully shipped through a private carrier. For a good general discussion of this topic review the analysis of The Gun Zone at "www.thegunzone.com".

338   A detailed listing of federal agencies may be found at the *LSU Libraries Federal Agency Directory: Alphabetical Directory*, which is on-line at "www.lib.lsu.edu/gov/alpha".

339   *See generally* 6 U.S.C. § 101 (mission objective of the Department of Homeland Security).

340   The Transportation Security Administration's website, at "www.tsa.gov", has comprehensive links to major air, rail, road, and sea carriers where these

restrictions may be found. Violation of these companies' policies regarding firearms would result, at best, in denial of boarding.

341   The federal statute prohibiting carrying a weapon onto an aircraft is 49 U.S.C. § 46505, which provides: "(a) In this section, 'loaded firearm' means a starter gun or a weapon designed or converted to expel a projectile through an explosive, that has a cartridge, a detonator, or powder in the chamber, magazine, cylinder, or clip. (b) An individual shall be fined under title 18, imprisoned for not more than 10 years, or both, if the individual (1) when on, or attempting to get on, an aircraft in, or intended for operation in, air transportation or intrastate air transportation, has on or about the individual or the property of the individual a concealed dangerous weapon that is or would be accessible to the individual in flight; (2) has placed, attempted to place, or attempted to have placed a loaded firearm on that aircraft in property not accessible to passengers in flight; or (3) has on or about the individual, or has placed, attempted to place, or attempted to have placed on that aircraft, an explosive or incendiary device."

342   The federal statute regarding terrorist acts against mass transportation vehicles is 18 U.S.C. § 1993, and provides: "(a) Whoever willfully . . . . (2) places or causes to be placed any biological agent or toxin for use as a weapon, destructive substance, or destructive device in, upon, or near a mass transportation vehicle or ferry, without previously obtaining the permission of the mass transportation provider, and with the intent to endanger the safety of any passenger or employee of the mass transportation provider, or with reckless disregard for the safety of human life . . . ."

343   The federal statute defining a "destructive device" is 18 U.S.C. § 921(a)(4), and provides: "(4) The term 'destructive device' means (A) any explosive, incendiary, or poison gas (i) bomb, (ii) gernade, (iii) rocket having a propellant charge of more than four ounces, (iv) missile having an explosive or incendiary charge of more than one-quarter ounce, (v) mine, or (vi) device similar to any of the devices in the preceding clauses; (B) any type of weapon (other than a shotgun or a shotgun shell which the Secretary finds is generally recognized as particularly suitable for sporting purposes) by whatever name known which will, or which may be readily converted to, expel a projectile by the action of an explosive or other propellant, and which has any barrel with a bore of more than one-half inch . . . ."

344   18 U.S.C. § 1993(a)(8) (person who places or causes to be placed a destructive device near or in a mass transportation vehicle shall be fined or imprisoned more than twenty years or both).

345   *See Wilhoite v. Melvin Simon & Associates, Inc.*, 640 N.E.2d 382, 385 (Ind.Ct.App. 1994), *citing Marrone v. Washington Jockey Club*, 227 U.S. 633 (1912).

346   *See, e.g., Barbre v. Indianapolis Water Co.*, 400 N.E.2d 1142, 1145 (Ind.Ct.App. 1980) (a person entering the land of another comes onto the land as an invitee, licensee, or trespasser).

347   *See, e.g., Industrial Disposal Corporation of America*, 407 N.E.2d at 1205 (a license merely confers a privilege to do some act or acts on the land without possessing a real property estate therein).

348   *See, e.g., Schrum v. Moskaluk*, 655 N.E.2d 561, 565 (Ind.Ct.App. 1995).

349   *See generally Markle v. Hacienda Mexican Restaurant*, 570 N.E.2d 969, 974 (Ind.Ct.App. 1991) (employee is an invitee).

350   *See, e.g., Remington Freight Lines, Inc. v. Larkey*, 644 N.E.2d 931, 939-940 (Ind.Ct.App. 1994) (Indiana recognizes the distinction between employees who are retained for a definite duration or subject to contract, and employees whose employment is of indefinite duration, and may be terminated at the will of the employer for any reason; and this distinction is between a contractual and at will employee and is of import for purposes of termination).

351   *See generally Hire v. Pinkerton*, 127 N.E.2d 244 (Ind.Ct.App. 1955) (general discussion of civil tort of trespass).

352   The Indiana statute on criminal trespass is IC 35-43-2-2, which provides: "(a) A person who: (1) not having a contractual interest in the property, knowingly or intentionally enters the real property of another person after having denied entry by the other person or that person's agent; (2) not having a contractual interest in the property, knowingly or intentionally refuses to leave the real property

of another person after having been asked to leave by the other person or that person's agent; (3) accompanies another person in a vehicle, with knowledge that the other person knowingly or intentionally is exerting unauthorized control over the vehicle; (4) knowingly or intentionally interferes with the possession or use of the property of another person without the person's consent; (5) not having a contractual interest in the property, knowingly or intentionally enters the dwelling of another person without the person's consent; or (6) knowingly or intentionally: (A) travels by train without lawful authority or the railroad carrier's consent; and (B) rides on the outside of a train or inside a passenger car, locomotive, or freight car, including a boxcar, flatbed, or container without lawful authority or the railroad carrier's consent; commits criminal trespass, a Class A misdemeanor. However, the offense if a Class D felony if it is committed on a scientific research facility, on school property, or on a school bus or the person has a prior unrelated conviction for an offense under this section concerning the same property. (b) A person has been denied entry under subdivision (a)(1) of this section when the person has been denied entry by means of: (1) personal communication, oral or written; or (2) posting or exhibiting a notice at the main entrance in a manner that is either prescribed by law or likely to come to the attention of the public. . . ."

353   *See generally Gibson v. Review Board of the Indiana Department of Workforce Development*, 671 N.E.2d 933, 937-38 (Ind.Ct.App. 1996) (Indiana case comparing and contrasting use of force cases on a spectrum, from justified to unjustified).

354   The statute for legal authority to engage in conduct that would otherwise be criminal is codified at IC 35-41-3-1, which provides: "A person is justified in engaging in conduct otherwise prohibited if he has legal authority to do so."

355   *See generally Eukers v. State*, 728 N.E.2d 219, 223 (Ind.Ct.App. 2000) (function of prosecutor to investigate crimes and bring criminal charges, but legislature has vested prosecutor with inherent power to bring or dismiss charges).

356   IC 35-41-3-1 (legal authority to do what would otherwise be a criminal act).

357   *See Carroll v. State*, 744 N.E.2d 432, 433 (Ind. 2001) (Indiana Supreme Court general discussion of use of force and deadly force).

358   *See Wilcher v. State*, 771 N.E.2d 113, 116 (Ind.Ct.App. 2002) (enumeration of the elements of a successful self-defense claim to homicide).

359   *See generally Geralds v. State*, 647 N.E.2d 369, 373 (Ind.Ct.App. 1995) (reasonableness fear of harm is a question of factual circumstances).

360   *See Mariscal v. State*, 687 N.E.2d 378, 381 (Ind.Ct.App. 1997) (burden of proof, once affirmative defense of self-defense is raised, is on state).

361   *See Brown v. State*, 738 N.E.2d 271, 273 (Ind. 2000) (State may rebut self-defense claim directly, or by simply relying upon the sufficiency of evidence in chief).

362   That statute creating a legal justification for the use of force, including deadly force, is IC 35-41-3-2, which provides as follows: "(a)   A person is justified in using reasonable force against another person to protect the person or a third person from what the person reasonably believes to be the imminent use of unlawful force. However, a person is justified in using deadly force only if the person reasonably believes that that force is necessary to prevent serious bodily injury to the person or a third person or the commission of a forcible felony. No person in this state shall be placed in jeopardy of any kind whatsoever for protecting the person or a third person by reasonable means necessary.(b) A person is justified in using reasonable force, including deadly force, against another person if the person reasonably believes that the force is necessary to prevent or terminate the other person's unlawful entry of or attack on the person's dwelling or curtilage.(c) With respect to property other than a dwelling or curtilage, a person is justified in using reasonable force against another person if the person reasonably believes that the force is necessary to immediately prevent or terminate the other person's trespass on or criminal interference with property lawfully in the person's possession, lawfully in possession of a member of the person's immediate family, or belonging to a person whose property the person has authority to protect. However, a person is not justified in using deadly force unless that force is justified under subsection (a). (d) A person is justified in using reasonable force, including deadly force, against another person if the person reasonably believes that the force is necessary to prevent or stop the other person from hijacking, attempting to hijack, or otherwise seizing or attempting to seize unlawful control of an aircraft in flight. For purposes of this subjection, an aircraft is considered to be in flight while the

aircraft is: (1) on the ground in Indiana: (A) after the doors of the aircraft are closed for takeoff; and (B) until the aircraft takes off; (2) in the airspace above Indiana; or (3) on the ground in Indiana: (A) after the aircraft lands; and (B) before the doors of the aircraft are opened after landing. (e) Notwithstanding subsections (a), (b), and (c), a person is not justified in using force if: (1) the person is committing or is escaping after the commission of a crime; (2) the person provokes unlawful action by another person with intent to cause bodily injury to the other person; or (3) the person has entered into combat with another person or is the initial aggressor unless the person withdraws from the encounter and communicates to the other person the intent to do so and the other person nevertheless continues or threatens to continue unlawful action.(f) Notwithstanding subsection (d), a person is not justified in using force if the person: (1) is committing, or is escaping after the commission of, a crime; (2) provokes unlawful action by another person, with intent to cause bodily injury to the other person; or (3) continues to combat another person after the other person withdraws from the encounter and communicates the other person's intent to stop hijacking, attempting to hijack, or otherwise seizing or attempting to seize unlawful control of an aircraft in flight."

363   IC 35-41-3-2(a) (use of force is justified to protect person or third person from imminent unlawful force).

364   *Id.*

365   *Id.*

366   The statute defining the term "serious bodily injury" is IC 35-41-1-25, and provides: "'Serious bodily injury' means bodily injury that creates a substantial risk of death or that causes: (1) serious permanent disfigurement; (2) unconsciousness; (3) extreme pain; (4) permanent or protracted loss or impairment of the function of a bodily member or organ; or (5) loss of a fetus."

367   The statute defining the terms "forcible felony" is IC 35-41-1-11, and provides: "'Forcible Felony' means a felony that involves the use or threat of force against a human being, or in which there is imminent danger of bodily injury to a human being."

368   IC 35-41-3-2(b) (use of reasonable force is justified, including deadly

force, if a person reasonably believes that force is necessary to prevent or terminate unlawful entry or attack on dwelling or curtilage).

369   IC 35-41-1-10 (definition of dwelling for penal code).

370   *See Fox v. State*, 384 N.E.2d 1159, 1163 (Ind.Ct.App. 1979).

371   *See generally State v. Bugg*, 66 Kan. 668, 72 P. 236, 237 (1903) (curtilage includes all buildings in close proximity to the dwelling, which are continually used for the carrying on of domestic employment).

372   IC 35-41-3-2(c) (person justified in using non-deadly force to protect property other than dwelling or curtliage).

373   IC 35-41-3-2(a)(b)(c) (unless authorized to protect person, third party, dwelling, or curtliage, deadly force is not justified to protect other property).

374   IC 35-41-3-2(d) (reasonable force, including deadly force, justified to protect hijacked airliner and passengers over Indiana).

375   The statute regarding use of force to effectuate arrest or prevent escape is IC 35-41-3-3, and provides: "(a)   A person other than a law enforcement officer is justified in using reasonable force against another person to effect an arrest or prevent the other person's escape if: (1) a felony has been committed; and (2) there is probable cause to believe the other person committed that felony. However, such a person is not justified in using deadly force unless that force is justified under . . . [IC 31-41-3-2]. (b)   A law enforcement officer is justified in using reasonable force if the officer reasonably believes that the force is necessary to effect lawful arrest. However, an officer is justified in using deadly force only if the officer: (1) has probable cause to believe that that deadly force is necessary: (A) to prevent the commission of a forcible felony; or (B) to effect an arrest of a person who the officer has probable cause to believe poses a threat of serious bodily injury to the officer or a third person; and (2) has given a warning, if feasible, to the person against whom the deadly force is to be used.(c) A law enforcement officer making an arrest under an invalid warrant is justified in using force as if the warrant was valid, unless the officer knows that the warrant is invalid. (d) A law enforcement

officer who has an arrested person in custody is justified in using the same force to prevent the escape of the arrested person from custody that the officer would be justified in using if the officer was arresting that person. However, an officer is justified in using deadly force only if the officer: (1) has probable cause to believe that deadly force is necessary to prevent the escape from custody of a person who the officer has probable cause to believe poses a threat of serious bodily injury to the officer or a third person; and (2) has given a warning, if feasible, to the person against whom the deadly force is to be used. (e) A guard or other official in a penal facility or a law enforcement officer is justified in using reasonable force, including deadly force, if the officer has probable cause to believe that the force is necessary to prevent the escape of a person who is detained in the penal facility. (f) Notwithstanding subsection (b), (d), or (e), a law enforcement officer who is a defendant in a criminal prosecution has the same right as a person who is not a law enforcement officer to assert self-defense under IC 35-41-3-2."

376   IC 35-41-3-2(e)(f) (exceptions to the legal justification, whereby affirmative defense is inapplicable).

377   IC 35-41-3-2(e)(1) (no legal justification for using force if person is committing or escaping after commission of crime).

378   IC 35-41-3-2(e)(2) (no legal justification for using force if person provokes unlawful action by another with intent to cause bodily injury to the other person).

379   IC 35-41-3-2(e)(3) (no legal justification if person entered into combat unless withdrawal and communication of intent to withdraw).

380   IC 35-41-3-2(f)(1)(2)(3) (no legal justification for use of force if hijacker communicates intent to stop hijacking).

381   The Indiana statute codifying the crime of murder is IC 35-42-1-1, and provides: "A person who: (1) knowingly or intentionally kills another human being; (2) kills another human being while committing or attempting to commit arson, burglary, child molesting, consumer product tampering, criminal deviate conduct, kidnaping, rape, robbery, or carjacking; (3) kills another human being while committing or attempting to commit: (A) dealing in or manufacturing

cocaine, a narcotic drug, or methamphetamine; (B) dealing in a schedule I, II, or III controlled substance; (C) dealing in a schedule IV controlled substance; (D) dealing with a schedule V controlled substance; or (4) knowingly or intentionally kills a fetus that has attained viability; commits murder, a felony."

382   The statute codifying voluntary manslaughter is codified at IC 35-42-1-3, and provides: "(a)   A person who knowingly or intentionally: (1) kills another human being; or (2) kills a fetus that has attained viability; while acting under sudden heat commits voluntary manslaughter, a Class B felony. However, the offense is a Class A felony if it is committed by means of a deadly weapon. (b) The existence of sudden heat is a mitigating factor that reduces what otherwise would be murder . . .to voluntary manslaughter."

383   The statute codifying involuntary manslaughter is codified at IC 35-42-1-4, and provides: "(a) As used in this section, "child care provider" means a person who provides child care in or on behalf of: (1) a child care center; or (2) a child care home; regardless of whether the child care center or child care home is licensed. (b)   As used in this section, "fetus" means a fetus that has attained viability.(c) A person who kills another human being while committing or attempting to commit: (1) a Class C or Class D felony that inherently poses a risk of serious bodily injury; (2) a Class A misdemeanor that inherently poses a risk of serious bodily injury; or (3) battery; commits involuntary manslaughter, a Class C felony. However, if the killing results from the operation of a vehicle, the offense is a Class D felony.(d)   A person who kills a fetus while committing or attempting to commit: (1) a Class C or Class D felony that inherently poses a risk of serious bodily injury; (2) a Class A misdemeanor that inherently poses a risk of serious bodily injury; or (3) battery; commits involuntary manslaughter, a Class C felony. However, if the killing results from the operation of a vehicle, the offense is a Class D felony. (e)   If: (1) a child care provider recklessly supervises a child; and (2) the child dies as a result of the child care provider's reckless supervision; the child care provider commits involuntary manslaughter, a Class D felony."

384   The statute codifying reckless homicide is IC 35-42-1-5, and provides: " A person who recklessly kills another human being commits reckless homicide, a Class C felony."

385   The statute codifying battery is IC 35-42-2-1, and provides: "(a) A person

who knowingly or intentionally touches another person in a rude, insolent, or angry manner commits battery, a Class B misdemeanor. However, the offense is: (1) a Class A misdemeanor if: (A) it results in bodily injury to any other person; (B) it is committed against a law enforcement officer or against a person summoned and directed by the officer while the officer is engaged in the execution of his official duty; (C) it is committed against an employee of a penal facility or juvenile detention facility (as defined in IC 31-9-2-1-71) while the employee is engaged in the execution of the employee's official duty; (D) it is committed against a firefighter (as defined in IC 9-18-34-1) while the firefighter is engaged in the execution of the firefighter's official duty; or (E) it is committed against a community policing officer volunteer: (i) while the volunteer is performing the duties described in IC 35-41-1-4.7; or (ii) because the person is a community policing volunteer; (2) a Class D felony if it results in bodily injury to: (A) a law enforcement officer or a person summoned and directed by the law enforcement officer while the officer is engaged in the execution of his official duty; (B) a person less than fourteen (14) years of age and is committed by a person at least eighteen (18) years of age; (C) a person of any age who is mentally or physically disabled and is committed by a person having the care of the mentally or physically disabled person, whether the care is assumed voluntarily or because of a legal obligation; (D) the other person and the person who commits the battery was previously convicted of a battery in which the victim was the other person; (E) an endangered adult (as defined in IC 12-10-3-2); (F) an employee of the department of correction while the employee is engaged in the execution of the employee's official duty; (G) an employee of a school corporation while the employee is engaged in the execution of the employee's official duty; (H) a correctional professional while the correctional professional is engaged in the execution of the correctional professional's official duty; (I) a person who is a health care provider (as defined in IC 16-18-2-163) while the health care provider is engaged in the execution of the health care provider's official duty; (J) an employee of a penal facility of juvenile detention facility (as defined in IC-31-9-2-71) while the employee is engaged in the execution of the employee's official duty; (K) a firefighter (as defined in IC 9-18-34-1) while the firefighter is engaged in the execution of the firefighter's official duty; or (L) a community policing volunteer: (i) while the volunteer is performing the duties described in IC 35-41-1-4.7; (or) (ii) because the person is a community policing volunteer; (3) a Class C felony if it results in serious bodily injury to any other person of if it is committed by means of a deadly weapon; (4) a Class B felony if it results in serious bodily injury to a person less than fourteen (14) years of age and is committed by a person at least eighteen (18) years of age; (5) a Class A felony if it results in the death of a person less than fourteen (14) years of age and is committed by a person at least eighteen (18) years of age; (6) a Class C felony if it results in serious bodily injury to an endangered adult (as defined in IC 12-10-3-2); and (7) a Class B felony if it results in the death of an endangered adult (as defined in IC 12-10-3-2). (b) For purposes of this section: (1) 'law enforcement officer' includes an alcoholic beverage enforcement officer; and (2) a 'correctional professional' means a: (A) probation officer; (B) parole officer; (C) community corrections worker; or (D) home detention officer."

386   Aggravated battery is defined and codified at IC 35-42-2-1.5, and provides: "A person who knowingly or intentionally inflicts injury on a person that creates a substantial risk of death or causes: (1) serious permanent disfigurement; (2) protracted loss or impairment of the function of a bodily member or organ; or (3) the loss of a fetus; commits aggravated battery, a Class B felony."

387   Domestic battery is defined in IC 35-42-2-1.3, and provides: "(a) A person who knowingly or intentionally touches an individual who: (1) is or was a spouse of the other person; (2) is or was living as if a spouse of the other person as provided in subsection (b); or (3) has a child in common with the other person; in a rude insolent, or angry manner that results in bodily injury to the person described in subdivision (1), (2), or (3) commits domestic battery, a Class A misdemeanor. However, the offense is a Class D felony if the person has a previous, unrelated conviction under this section (or IC 35-42-2-1(a)(2)(E) before its repeal). (b) In considering whether a person is or was living as a spouse of another individual in subsection (a)(2), the court shall review the following: (1) the duration of the relationship; (2) the frequency of contact; (3) the financial interdependence; (4) whether the two (2) individuals are raising children together; (5) whether the two (2) individuals have engaged in tasks directed toward maintaining a common household; and (6) other factors the court considers relevant."

388   The crime of criminal recklessness if codified at IC35-42-2-2, and provides: "(a) As used in this section, 'hazing' means forcing or requiring another person: (1) with or without the consent of the other person; and (2) as a condition of association with a group or organization; to perform an act that creates a substantial risk of bodily injury. (b) A person who recklessly, knowingly, or intentionally performs: (1) an act that creates a substantial risk of bodily injury to another person; or hazing; commits criminal recklessness. Except as provided in subsection (c), criminal recklessness is a Class B misdemeanor. (c) The offense of criminal recklessness as defined in subsection (b) is: (1) a Class A

misdemeanor if the conduct includes the use of a vehicle; (2) a Class D felony if it is committed while armed with a deadly weapon; or (3) a Class C felony if it is committed by shooting a firearm from a vehicle into an inhabited dwelling or other building or place where people are likely to gather. (d) A person who recklessly, knowingly, or intentionally: (1) inflicts serious bodily injury on another person; or (2) performs hazing that results in serious bodily injury to a person; commits criminal recklessness, a Class D felony. However, the offense is a Class C felony if committed by means of a deadly weapon. (e) A person, other than a person who has committed an offense under this section or a delinquent act that would be an offense under this section if the violator was an adult, who: (1) makes a report of hazing in good faith; (2) participates in good faith in a judicial proceeding resulting from a report hazing; (3) employs a reporting or participating person described in subdivision in (1) or (2); or (4) supervises a reporting or participating person described in subdivision (1) or (2); is not liable for civil damages or criminal penalties that might otherwise be imposed because of the report or participation. (f) A person described in subsection (e)(1) or (e)(2) is presumed to act in good faith. (g) A person described in subsection (e)(1) or (e)(2) may not be treated as acting in bad faith solely because the person did not have probable cause to believe that a person committed: (1) an offense under this section; or (2) a delinquent act that would be an offense under this section if the offender was an adult."

389   This was determined by the author's Westlaw on-line researching of Indiana caselaw.

390   *See generally Baker v. Finneman & Brown Properties, L.L.C.*, 793 N.E.2d 1203, 1206-09 (Ind.Ct.App. 2003) (discussion of common law duty to provide aid).

391   *See generally Miranda v. Arizona*, 384 U.S. 436, 86 S.Ct. 1602, 16 L.Ed.2d 694 (1966) (seminal case that holds that prosecution may not use statements unless it demonstrates that use of certain procedural safeguards effective to preserve the privilege against self-incrimination).

392   *See generally Frazier v. Cupp,* 394 U.S. 731, 89 S.Ct. 1420, 22 L.Ed.2d684 (1969) (the fact that police officers lied to defendant that an accomplice had been arrested and made confession, did not render the confession involuntary); *see also Patterson v. State*, 563 N.E.2d 653 (Ind.Ct.App. 1990); *Cater v. State*, 490 N.E.2d 288 (Ind. 1986).

393   The most recognized expert on the coercive nature of police interrogations is Dr. Richard Ofshe.

394   *See Eukers,* 728 N.E.2d at 223 (prosecutorial discretion).

395   *See Wurster v. State,* 715 N.E.2d 341, 346 (Ind. 1999) (duty of grand jury is to diligently inquire, to obtain legal evidence, to discover and detect crime); *see also Sanchez v. Indiana,* 732 N.E.2d 165, 171 (Ind.Ct.App. 2000) (transfer granted, but case is significant in that it addresses historical underpinnings of grand jury).

396   *See generally Minton v. State,* 802 N.E.2d 929, 936 (Ind.Ct.App. 2004) (discussion of double jeopardy clause under Indiana and federal constitution).

397   *See generally Byrd v. AFSCME,* 781 N.E.2d 713, 729-30 (Ind.Ct.App. 2003) (burden of proof applicable to civil case in general is preponderance).

398   *See Sans v. Monticello Insurance Company,* 676 N.E.2d 1099, 1101 (Ind.Ct.App. 1997) (Indiana courts have long upheld standard exclusionary clauses for the insured's intentional acts as in furtherance of public policy that a person should not be able to insure against harms he may cause others).

399   *See, e.g.,* Wiley Clapp, *Concealed Carry: The Shooter's Guide to Selecting Handguns* (2002).

400   *See* Paxton Quigley, *Armed and Female: Twelve Million American Women Own Guns, Should You?* (1990).

401   The statute allowing for a citizen's arrest is IC 35-33-1-4, which provides: "(a) Any person may arrest any other person if: (1) the other person committed a felony in his presence; (2) a felony has been committed and he has probable cause to believe that the other person has committed that felony; or (3) a misdemeanor involving a breach of peace is being committed in his presence and the arrest is necessary to prevent the continuance of the breach of peace. (b) A person making an arrest under this section shall, as soon as practical, notify a law enforcement officer and deliver custody of the person arrested to a law enforcement officer. (c) The law enforcement officer may process the arrested person as if the officer had

arrested him. The officer who receives or processes a person arrested by another under this section is not liable for false arrest or false imprisonment."

402   *See* Chapters 4 to 13 (limitations on carrying a handgun with a license).

403   *See* Chapter 3 (state-to-state reciprocity).

404   As previously noted, handguns may not be shipped through U.S. mail. They must be lawfully shipped through a private carrier.

405   *See* IC 35-47-10-1, *et seq.*

406   IC 35-47-2-4 (Superintendent may adopt rules imposing limitations on the use and carrying of handguns carried in the scope of employment).

407   *See* ATF 4473 form (form completed when purchasing and/or transferring a handgun).

408   *See Estate of Heck,* 786 N.E.2d at 270 (duty in storage of firearms).

409   *See* House Bill No. 1349.

410   *See* Article I § 32 of the Indiana Constitution (Indiana's constitutional right to keep and bear arms).

411   *See* IC 35-47-11-1 (only Legislature can enact firearms regulations, but there is a narrow exception for qualified disasters).

412   The statute regarding conditions warranting an emergency ordinance is IC 35-47-11-3, which provides: "The legislative body of a unit may adopt an emergency ordinance under this chapter if: (1) a disaster (as defined by IC 10-14-3-1) has occurred or is likely to occur in the unit; and (2) a local disaster emergency has been declared in the unit under IC 10-14-3-29."

413   The statute allowing adoption of an emergency ordinance and procedures is   IC 35-47-11-4, which provides: "Notwithstanding any other law, if the conditions described under section 3 of this chapter are present within a unit, the legislative body of the unit may adopt an emergency ordinance under this chapter: (1) without complying with the public notice and public meeting provisions of: (A) IC 5-14-1.5; or (B) any other statute; (2) on the same day that the ordinance is presented to the legislative body; and (3) by a majority vote of the members of the legislative body."

414   The statute providing for an executive of a municipality to adopt an emergency ordinance if the legislative body cannot be convened is IC 35-47-11-6, which provides: "If: (1) the conditions described under section 3 of this chapter are present within a unit; (2) an unsuccessful attempt is made to convene the legislative body for the purpose of adopting an emergency ordinance under this chapter; and (3) in the case of a municipality, an unsuccessful attempt is made to convene the works board to act under this chapter as if the works board were the legislative body; the executive of a municipality or the presiding officer of a county executive may declare a restriction on the sale of firearms anywhere within the unit for a period of not more than seventy-two (72) hours after the restriction is declared. A declaration under this section has the same effect as an ordinance adopted under section 4 of this chapter and becomes effective and expires as provided in section 5 of this chapter."

415   The statute allowing for a seventy-two (72) hour ban on the sale of weapons in qualified disasters is IC 35-47-11-5, which provides: "An emergency ordinance adopted under Section 4 of this chapter: (1) takes effect on the date and at the time of the adoption of the ordinance; and (2) expires the earlier of : (A) seventy-two (72) hours after the time of the adoption of the ordinance; or (B) a time specified in the emergency ordinance."

416   *See Dozier*, 709 N.E.2d at 31 (Legislature has power in the interest of public safety to provide reasonable regulations on handguns).

417   The statute that precludes the possession of armor-piercing handgun ammunition is IC 35-47-5-11, which provides: "(a) As used in this section, 'armor-piercing handgun ammunition' means a cartridge that: (1) can be fired in a handgun; and (2) will, upon firing, expel a projectile that has a metal core and an outer

coating of plastic. (b) a person who knowingly or intentionally: (1) manufactures; (2) possesses; (3) transfers possession of; (4) offers to transfer possession of; armor-piercing handgun ammunition commits a Class C felony. (c) This section does not apply to nylon coated ammunition, plastic shot capsules, or ammunition designed to be used in rifles or shotguns. (d) This section does not apply to a law enforcement officer who is acting in the course of the officer's official duties or to a person who manufactures or imports for sale or sells armor-piercing ammunition to a law enforcement agency."

418   18 U.S.C. § 929(a)(1) (person who uses armor piercing ammunition shall, in addition to the crime, be sentenced to a term of imprisonment for not less than five years).

419   18 U.S.C. § 922(a)(7) (illegal for any person to manufacture or import armor piercing ammunition, except for law enforcement or military uses).

420   The statute defining the term "armor piercing ammunition" is 18 U.S.C. § 921(a)(17)(B) (ammunition with a projectile or projectile core constructed entirely of one or a combination of tungsten alloys, steel, iron, brass, bronze, beryllium copper, or depleted uranium).

421   IC 35-47-11-2 (a unit may not regulate in any measure the ownership, possession, sale, transfer, or transportation of firearms).

422   35-47-11-5 (local government can suspend firearms sales for seventy-two hours in qualified emergency).

423   IC 35-47-11-2 (local government can regulate firearms on property it owns, possesses, or administers).

424   IC 35-47-2-1(a) (carry without a license is permitted in one's dwelling, property or fixed place of business).

425   IC 35-47-2-4 (handgun permits types and application and license fees).

426   *Id.*

427   IC 35-47-2-3(a) (handgun application statute).

428   *See Kellogg v. City of Gary*, 562 N.E.2d 685 (Ind.1990) (local police department cannot simply refuse to make handgun permit applications available).

429   IC 35-47-2-4(b) ($5.00 for replacement license).

430   IC 35-47-2-2 (transportation in a secure wrapper).

431   IC 35-47-2-3(e) (license issued shall be valid for a period of four years from date of issuance).

432   *See* Chapter 3 (handgun reciprocity).

433   *See* Chapter 11 (weapons banned on federal property).

434   *See* Chapter 12 (weapons restrictions on mass transportation).

435   *See* Chapter 13 (carrying a handgun on private property).

436   *See* IC 35-47-2-1, *et seq.* (carrying a handgun statutes).

437   *See* Chapter 13 (carrying a handgun on private property).

438   *Id.*

439   *See* IC 35-47-2-1 *et seq.* (handgun licensing statutory scheme).

440   The administrative code section applicable to handguns and deer hunting is 312 IAC 9-3-3, which provides: "(2) A handgun must: (A) conform to the requirements of IC 35-47-2; (B) have a barrel at least four (4) inches long; and (C) fire

a bullet of .243 inch diameter or larger. All 38 special ammunition is prohibited. The handgun cartridge case, without bullet, must be at least one and sixteen-hundredths (1.16) inches long. A handgun must not be concealed. Full metal jacketed bullets are unlawful. A handgun may be possessed in the field outside lawful shooting hours only if there are no shells in the chamber or magazine. All 25/20, 32/20, 30 carbine, and 38 special ammunition is prohibited."

441   IC 35-47-2-1 (person shall not carry without a license in his/her possession).

442   18 U.S.C. §922(g) (after notice and hearing of protective order, it is a federal criminal violation to purchase, receive, or possess a firearm while the order is in effect).

443   IC 35-47-2-1(b) (person with a conviction for domestic battery may not possess a firearm unless that person's rights have been restored).

444   IC 35-47-4-5 (serious violent felon cannot possess a firearm).

445   IC 35-47-4-3, provides: "(a) This section does not apply to a law enforcement officer who is acting within the scope of the law enforcement officer's official duties or to a person who is justified in using reasonable force against another person under: (1) IC 35-41-3-2; or (2) IC 35-41-3-3. (b) A person who knowingly or intentionally points a firearm at another person commits a Class D felony. However, the offense is a Class A misdemeanor if the firearm was not loaded."

446   IC 35-41-3-2(a) (a person is justified in using force, including deadly force, if the person reasonably believes that the force is necessary to prevent serious bodily injury to the person or a third person or the commission of a forcible felony).

447   IC 35-41-3-2(b) (a person is justified in using force, including deadly force, if the person reasonably believes the force is necessary to prevent or terminate the other person's unlawful entry of or attack on the person's dwelling or curtilage).

448   IC 35-41-3-2(d) (a person is justified in using force, including deadly force, if the person reasonably believes the force is necessary to prevent or stop a hijacking

of an aircraft in Indiana).

449   One potential crime for such activity may be tampering with evidence and obstruction of justice pursuant to IC 35-44-2-4, which provides: "(a) A person who: . . . .(3) alters, damages, or removes any record, document, or thing, with intent to prevent it from being produced or used as evidence in any official proceeding or investigation . . . .commits obstruction of justice, a Class D felony."

450   *See Sans,* 676 N.E.2d at 1101 (intentional tort exclusions to standard insurance policies).

ORDER FORM

Indiana Handgun Law, 2005 Edition

Please send _____ copies of *Indiana Handgun Law, 2005 Edition* at $22.95 per copy, plus sales tax of $1.38, and $3.95 per copy shipping and handling ($28.28 total per copy).

Ship to:

Name: _____

Address: _____

City: _____

State: _____

Zip Code: _____

E-Mail: _____

Payment Type: (payable to: Ciyou & Dixon, P.C.)

_____ **Check/Money Order**

_____ **Visa**

_____ **MasterCard**

_____ **American Express**

_____ **Discover**

Credit Card Number (if applicable):

_____

Expiration Date: _____

Signature: _____

Mail with Payment to: **Ciyou & Dixon, P.C., 320 North Meridian Street, Suite 311, Indianapolis, Indiana 46204**

SUGGESTIONS FOR 2006 EDITION

In future editions of *Indiana Handgun Law,* I would like to see the following topics/issues addressed:

1. _____

2. _____

3. _____

4. _____

5. _____

6. _____

7. _____

8. _____

9. _____

10. _____

Mail to: **Ciyou & Dixon, P.C., 320 North Meridian Street, Suite 311, Indianapolis, Indiana 46204**

NEW FOR THE 2006 EDITION

Several new or expanded coverages are planned for the 2006 edition as the 2006 Edition of the Book goes to press. Some of those topics are:

- Major carry restrictions in reciprocal states;

- Reference appendices covering: (1) reciprocal states contact information; (2) enumeration of all Indiana gun crimes and crimes that may be enhanced with firearms; (3) references articles, books, and internet sites;

- Chapter addressing the substantial Indiana and federal restrictions associated with firearms' possession and protective and restraining orders;

- Chapter addressing minors and firearms laws;

- Developments on carry and possession by TSA;

- Expanded questions and answers;

- Chapter on history of firearms regulation;

- Glossary of terms; and

- New Indiana and federal statutory and caselaw.

THE AUTHOR

Bryan Lee Ciyou, 36, was born in Indianapolis, Indiana.

He has always taken the road less traveled. He grew up interested in the outdoors, firearms, travel, and anything a little different.

By his early 20s, he had spent time doing humanitarian aid work in politically unstable third world countries like Haiti, sometimes seeing first hand the dark, illicit and harmful side of firearms.

He graduated from Indiana University with distinction, and from the honors program, in 1991, with a Bachelor of Arts, and Indiana University Law School in 1994, *cum laude.*

As an attorney, he has handled many matters involving weapons, ranging from representing gun shops as corporate counsel to deadly force cases. Mr. Ciyou is admitted to the bars of Indiana, the Seventh Circuit, and the U.S. Supreme Court.

While published on a variety of legal topics that contribute to his professional and personal interests, Mr. Ciyou considers this Book his most significant written publication after a decade of private practice.

Significantly, this Book is the culmination of a lifetime of experiences and interests. It is written with the intense passion of a person who believes the 2nd Amendment is meaningful yet today.